CLAIM DENIED!

How to Appeal a VA Denial of Benefits

JOHN D. ROCHE

Potomac Books, Inc.
Washington, D.C.

Library of Congress Cataloging-in-Publication Data
Roche, John D., Maj.
Claim denied! : how to appeal a VA denial of benefits / John D. Roche. — 1st ed.
p. cm.
ISBN 978-1-59797-116-4 (pbk. : alk. paper)
1. Disabled veterans—Legal status, laws, etc.—United States—Popular works. 2. Veterans—Medical care—Law and legislation—United States—Popular works. 3. United States. Dept. of Veterans Affairs—Rules and practice—Popular works. 4. Administrative remedies—United States—Popular works. I. Title.
KF7713.R63 2008
343.73'011—dc22
2008031089

Printed in the United States of America on acid-free paper that meets the American National Standards Institute Z39-48 Standard.

Potomac Books, Inc.
22841 Quicksilver Drive
Dulles, Virginia 20166

First Edition

10 9 8 7 6 5 4 3 2

CONTENTS

ABBREVIATIONS

A&A	Aid and Attendance
ABCMR	Army Board for Correction of Military Records
ADJ	Adjudication
AFBCMR	Air Force Board for Correction of Military Records
AFSC	Air Force Specialty Code
AL	American Legion
ALJ	Administrative Law Judge
AMVETS	American Veterans
AO	Appeals Officer
AOJ	Agency of Original Jurisdiction
APP	Appeal
BCMR	Board of Corrections for Military Records Coast Guard
BCNR	Board for Correction of Naval Records
BVA	Board of Veterans' Appeals
"C"	Claim File Number
C&P	Compensation and Pension Evaluation
CAFC	United States Court of Appeals for the Federal Circuit
CAVC	United States Court of Appeals for Veterans Claims
CFR	Code of Federal Regulations

COMP	Compensation
CSS#	Claim File Number using Social Security Number
DAV	Disabled American Veterans
DEPS	Did Not Exist Prior to Service
DIC	Dependency Indemnity Compensation
DOD	Department of Defense
DOS	Date of Separation
DRG	Diagnostic Related Groups
DRO	Decision Review Officer
DSC	Direct Service Connection
DSMIV	Diagnostic and Statistical Manual of Mental Disorders
EOD	Entrance on Active Duty
EPS	Existed Prior to Service
FOIA	Freedom of Information Act
FR	Federal Register
GSW	Gun Shot Wound
HO	Regional Office Hearing Officer
IOM	Institute of Medicine
JAG	Judge Advocate General
KC	Korean Conflict
KIA	Killed in Action
KIA/BNR	Killed in Action/Body Not Recovered
LOD	Line of Duty
MIA	Missing in Action
MOAA	Military Officers Association of America
MOS	Military Occupational Specialty
MR	Morning Report
N/A	Not Applicable
NARA	National Archives and Records Administration
NAS	National Academy Science

NCOA	Non-Commissioned Officers Association
NOA	Notice of Appeal
NOD	Notice of Disagreement
NPRC	National Personnel Record Center
NSC-KC	Non-service connection Korean Conflict
NSC-VE	Non-service connection Vietnam Era
NSC-WWII	Non-service connection World War II
OGC	Office of General Counsel
OIG	Office Inspector General
P&T	Permanent and Total
PCS	Permanent Change of Station
PGW	Persian Gulf War (1992)
POW	Prisoner of War
POW/MIA	Prisoners of Wars /Missing In Action
PTSD	Post Traumatic Stress Disorder
RAD	Released from Active Duty
RO	Rating Officer
RO	Regional Office
SBP	Survivors Benefit Program
SC	Service Connection
SMC	Special Monthly Compensation
SOC	Statement of the Case
SSA	Social Security Administration
SSD	Social Security Disability
SSOC	Supplemental Statement of the Case
USC	United States Code Title 38
TDIU	Total Disability due to Individual Unemployability
TDY	Temporary Duty
USA	U.S. Army
USAF	U.S. Air Force
USC	U.S. Code
USCA	U.S. Code Annotated

USCG	U.S. Coast Guard
USMC	U.S. Marine Corps
USMJ	U.S. Code of Military Justice
USN	U.S.Navy
VA	Department of Veterans Affairs
VAF	Veterans Administration Forms
VAMC	Veterans Administration Medical Center
VBA	Veterans Benefits Administration
VE	Vietnam Era
VFW	Veterans of Foreign Wars
VHA	Veterans Health Administration
VSO	Veterans Service Organization
VVA	Vietnam Veterans of America
WAC	Women's Army Corps
WIA	Wounded in Action
WWI	World War I
WWII	World War II

TERMS

Advance on the Docket: A change in the order in which an appeal is reviewed and decided from the date when it would normally occur to an earlier date.

Agency of Original Jurisdiction (AOJ): The office where a claim originates.

Appeal: A request for a review of an Agency of Original Jurisdiction (AOJ) determination on a claim.

Appeal Team: Reviews Notices of Disagreements for veterans who disagree with a rating decision; the primary function is to expediently process appeals and remands.

Appellant: An individual who has appealed an AOJ claim.

Board: The Board of Veterans' Appeals.

Board Member: *See* Member of the Board.

Board of Veterans' Appeals (BVA): The part of VA that reviews benefit claims appeals and that issues decisions on those appeals.

BVA Hearing: A personal hearing, held at the BVA office in Washington, D.C., or at a regional office, that is conducted by a member of the Board. A BVA hearing can be held by videoconference from some regional offices (*see* Travel Board Hearing).

Claim: A request for veterans' benefits.

Claim Number: A number assigned by VA that identifies a person who has filed a claim; often called a "C-number."

Claims File: *See* Claims Folder.

Claims Folder: The file containing all documents concerning a veteran's claim or appeal.

Court of Veterans Appeals: *See* U.S. Court of Appeals for Veterans Claims.

Decision: The final product of the BVA's review of an appeal. Possible decisions are granting or denial of the benefit or benefits claimed, or remanding of the case to the AOJ for additional action.

Determination: A decision on a claim made at the AOJ.

Docket: A listing of appeals that have been filed with BVA. Appeals are listed in numerical order, called docket number order, based on when a VA Form 9 is received by VA.

Docket Number: The number assigned to an appeal when a VA Form 9 is received by VA. By law, cases are reviewed by the Board in docket number order.

File: *See* Claims Folder.

Hearing: A meeting, similar to an interview, between an appellant and an official from VA who will decide an appellant's case, during which testimony and other evidence supporting the case is presented. There are two types of personal hearings: Regional Office hearings (also called local office hearings) and BVA hearings.

Issue: A benefit sought on a claim or an appeal. For example, if an appeal seeks a decision on three different matters, the appeal is said to contain three issues.

Local Office Hearing: *See* Regional Office Hearing.

Member of the Board: An attorney, appointed by the secretary of veterans affairs and approved by the president, who decides veterans' benefit appeals.

Motion: A legal term used to describe a request that some specific action be taken.

Motion to Advance on the Docket: A request that BVA review and make a decision on an appeal sooner than when it normally would.

Motion to Reconsider: A request for BVA to review its decision on an appeal.

Notice of Disagreement (NOD): A written statement expressing dissatisfaction or disagreement with a local VA office's determination on a benefit claim. It must be filed within one year of the date of the Regional Office's decision.

Predetermination Team: On receipt of a claim, all evidence will be reviewed to determine whether there is a statutory or regulatory bar to entitlement or whether the claim should be referred to a rating team member for a decision.

Post-determination Team: This function addresses claims for accrued benefits, apportionments, original pension claims not requiring a rating, dependency issues, death pension claims, and other duties such as preparing notification letters.

Rating Team: A group that determines the nature and severity of a veteran's injury, whether the injury was incurred during active military duty, and whether the injury presently affects the veteran's day-to-day life.

Rating Officer (RO): A member of the Rating Team.

Regional Office (RO): A local VA office; there are fifty-eight VA Regional Offices throughout the United States and its territories. The RO decides whether to approve or deny a claim.

Regional Office Hearing: A personal hearing conducted by a DRO officer. A regional office hearing may be conducted in addition to a BVA hearing.

Remand: An appeal returned to the Regional Office or medical facility where the claim originated.

Representative: Someone familiar with the benefit claim process who assists claimants in the preparation and presentation of an appeal. Most representatives are Veterans Service Organization employees who specialize in veterans' benefit claims. Most states, commonwealths, and territories also have experienced representatives to assist veterans. Other individuals, such as lawyers and agents, may also serve as appeal representatives.

RO Hearing: *See* Regional Office Hearing.

Statement of the Case (SOC): Prepared by the AOJ, this is a summary of the evidence considered, as well as a listing of the laws and regulations used in deciding a benefit claim. It also provides information on the right to appeal an BVA.

Substantive Appeal: A completed VA Form 9.

Supplemental Statement of the Case (SSOC): A summary, similar to an SOC, that VA prepares if a VA Form 9 contains a new issue or presents new evidence and the benefit is still denied. A Supplemental Statement of the Case will also be provided after an appeal is returned (remanded) to the RO by the Board for new or additional action.

To File: To submit in writing a statement or form.

Travel Board Hearing: A personal hearing conducted at a VA regional office by a member of the Board.

Triage Team: Reviews all incoming mail, is responsible for setting up claim files on all new claims where the claimant has never previously claimed benefits, and is also responsible for expediting the claiming process for terminally ill veterans.

U.S. Court of Appeals for Veterans Claims: An independent judiciary that reviews appeals of BVA decisions.

VA Form 9: This form, which accompanies the SOC, formally initiates the appeal process.

Veterans Service Organization (VSO): An organization that represents the interests of veterans. Most Veterans Service Organizations have specific membership criteria, although membership is not usually required to obtain assistance with benefit claims or appeals.

CODE OF FEDERAL REGULATIONS

The Code of Federal Regulations (CFR) is the official record of rules that are followed by the departments and agencies of the federal goverment. For the purposes of this book, following are explanations of CFRs that apply to veteran claims and the appeals process.

The complete list and explanation of the Code of Federal Regulations can be found online.

38 CFR §3.103
Procedural due process and appellate rights

Every claimant has the right to written notice of the decision made on his or her claim, the right to a hearing, and the right of representation. . . . Claimants and their representatives are entitled to notice of any decision made by the VA that affects payment of benefits. The notice must state the decisions made, effective dates, the reasons for the decision, the right of the veteran to a hearing on any issue involved in the claim, the right of representation, and the right to appeal.

38 CFR §3.159
Department of Veterans Affairs assistance in developing claims

The VA is obligated to complete applications. This

substantial completion includes the claimant's name, his or her relationship to the veteran if applicable, sufficient service information for the VA to verify the claimed service, the benefit claimed and any medical conditions on which it is based, the claimant's signature, and (for claims of nonservice-connected disability or death pension and parents' dependency and indemnity compensation) a statement of income.

The VA also is obligated to accept "competent medical evidence" provided by a person who is qualified through education, training, or experience to offer medical diagnoses, statements, or opinions. "Competent medical evidence" may also mean statements showing sound medical principles found in medical treatises. It would also include statements contained in well-respected medical and scientific articles and research reports or analyses.

The VA also accepts "competent lay evidence," which is defined as evidence not requiring specialized education, training, or experience from the individual offering the evidence.

38 CFR §3.303
Principles relating to service connection

Service connection means that the facts, shown by evidence, establish that a veteran was injured or contracted a disease while serving in the armed forces, or if preexisting, was aggravated during service. Each disabling condition shown by a veteran's service records for which he or she seeks a service connection must be considered on the basis of the places, types, and circumstances of service. Determination of service connection is based on review of the entire evidence on record.

38 CFR §3.309

Disease subject to presumptive service connection

The VA has a list of chronic diseases that qualify for service connection, and these diseases must be shown as occurring or worsening during service. The veteran is expected to provide time limits under §3.307 following service in a period of war or following peacetime service on or after January 1, 1947 (provided provisions of §3.307 are also satisfied).

38 CFR §3.310

Proximate results, secondary condition

If the veteran has a nonservice-connected disease or injury that is made worse during military service and not owing to the natural progress of the disease, benefits may be granted. However, the VA will not concede that a nonservice-connected disease or injury was aggravated during a service unless the veteran has already established (by medical evidence) the level of aggravation. Then, current medical evidence must show that the level of severity increased specifically during service dates. The rating activity will be applied to determine the baseline (previously established level) and current levels of severity under the Schedule for Rating Disabilities (38 CFR §4).

38 CFR §3.321 (b) (1)

General rating considerations

This section refers to assignment of a schedular rating. A "schedular rating" determines how much the VA will compensate a veteran for service-connected injuries or diseases. An "extra-schedular disability rating" applies to veterans who are unemployable owing to their injuries or service-connected disease.

38 CFR §4.1
Essentials of evaluative rating

For any type of disease and injury occurring before or during military service, an "evaluative rating" is used to determine percentages of impairment. Basically this helps define how much earning capacity a veteran has lost because of disease and injury. Different degrees of disability determine how to compensate for lost working time, proportionate to the severity of disability.

The veteran is required to have accurate and descriptive medical examinations that prove the limitation of activity because of a disabling condition. Over a period of many years, a veteran's disability claim may require new ratings when laws change, new medical knowledge is available, and the veteran's condition changes. Every examination and evaluation of disability must be related to every previous one for the VA to understand the claimant's relevant history.

38 CFR §4.2
Interpretation of examination reports

Each disability must be considered from the point of view of the veteran working or seeking work. However, the VA employs different examiners who may view the evidence unlike the person who looked at it at an earlier time. Also, the examiner may find that a diagnosis is not supported by the report or that the report does not contain sufficient detail. If that occurs, the rating board returns the report to the veteran because the information is insufficient for a proper evalation. The rating board looks for a consistent picture so that the current rating accurately reflects the nature of the disability.

38 CFR §4.3
Resolution of reasonable doubt

After all facts and data are carefully considered, if there are any doubts regarding what the degree of disability should be, the claim should be resolved in favor of the veteran.

38 CFR §4.6
Evaluation of evidence

The Rating Board is required to consider all evidence presented in a veteran's claim. This includes thoroughly examining each piece of information to determine what "weight" it should be given in relation to each other piece. The Rating Board also reviews evidence in light of the established policies of the Department of Veterans Affairs to ensure that decisions will be equitable and follow the requirements of the law.

38 CFR §4.19
Age in service-connected claims

Age is a consideration for decisions regarding pensions. Otherwise, it may not be considered as a factor in evaluating service-connected claims, service-connected disability, total disability, or unemployability ratings.

38 CFR §4.21
Application of rating schedule

Many claims have unique circumstances and therefore are not "typical," and VA adjudicators are not expected in all cases to fully described grades of disabilities. Findings need to be sufficiently characteristic of the disease or disability, however, and must be coordinated with the established rating schedules in all instances.

38 CFR §4.23
Attitude of rating officers

Directly quoting the Code of Federal Regulations: "It is to be remembered that the majority of applicants are disabled persons who are seeking benefits of law to which they believe themselves entitled. In the exercise of his or her functions, rating officers must not allow their personal feelings to intrude; an antagonistic, critical, or even abusive attitude on the part of a claimant should not in any instance influence the officers in the handling of the case. Fairness and courtesy must at all times be shown to applicants by all employees whose duties bring them in contact, directly or indirectly, with the Department's claimants."

38 CFR §4.41
History of injury

For service-related injuries, the disabled veteran needs to be able to trace his or her medical history from the original injury to treatment to the current state of recovery. This timeline should include how long a disability continued because of the initial injury, subsequent periods of incapacity, and current treatment. For periods of incapacity, details should especially address delayed union, inflammation, swelling, drainage, or operative intervention. In the absence of clear-cut evidence of service-related injury, the veteran's disability may *not* be classified as of traumatic origin but rather as congenital (inherited), developmental, or the effects of a healed disease.

VA FORM 9

The form recreated below shows the information that must be completed in full for a substantive appeal. It is available online at www.va.gov/vaforms/va/pdf/VA9.pdf

APPEAL TO BOARD OF VETERANS' APPEALS

IMPORTANT: *Read the attached instructions before you fill out this form. VA also encourages you to get assistance from your representative in filling out this form.*

1. NAME OF VETERAN *(Last Name, First Name, Middle Initial)*	2. CLAIM FILE NO. *(Include prefix)* 3. INSURANCE FILE NO. OR LOAN NO.

4. I AM THE:
- ☐ VETERAN
- ☐ VETERAN'S CHILD
- ☐ OTHER *(Specify)*
- ☐ VETERAN'S WIDOW/ER
- ☐ VETERAN'S PARENT

5. TELEPHONE NUMBERS		6. MY ADDRESS IS: *(Number & Street or Post Office Box, City, State & ZIP Code)*
A. HOME *(Include Area Code)*	B. WORK *(Include Area Code)*	

7. IF I AM NOT THE VETERAN, MY NAME IS: *(Last Name, First Name, Middle Initial)*

continued on next page

continued from previous page

8. HEARING

IMPORTANT: *Read the information about this block in paragraph 6 of the attached instructions. This block is used to request a Board of Veterans' Appeals hearing. DO NOT USE THIS FORM TO REQUEST A HEARING BEFORE VA REGIONAL OFFICE PERSONNEL. Check one (and only one) of the following boxes:*

A. ☐ I DO NOT WANT A BVA HEARING.

B. ☐ I WANT A BVA HEARING IN WASHINGTON, DC.

C. ☐ I WANT A BVA HEARING AT A LOCAL VA OFFICE BEFORE A MEMBER, OR MEMBERS, OF THE BVA.
(Not available at Washington, DC, or Baltimore, MD, Regional Offices.)

---

9. THESE ARE THE ISSUES I WANT TO APPEAL TO THE BVA: *(Be sure to read the information about this block in paragraph 6 of the attached instructions.)*

A. ☐ I WANT TO APPEAL ALL OF THE ISSUES LISTED ON THE STATEMENT OF THE CASE AND ANY SUPPLEMENTAL STATEMENTS OF THE CASE THAT MY LOCAL VA OFFICE SENT TO ME.

B. ☐ I HAVE READ THE STATEMENT OF THE CASE AND ANY SUPPLEMENTAL STATEMENT OF THE CASE I RECEIVED. I AM ONLY APPEALING THESE ISSUES:
(List below.)

---

10. HERE IS WHY I THINK THAT VA DECIDED MY CASE INCORRECTLY: *(Be sure to read the information about this block in paragraph 6 of the attached instructions.)*

(Continue on the back, or attach sheets of paper, if you need more space.)

---

11. SIGNATURE OF PERSON MAKING THIS APPEAL	12. DATE *(MM/DD/YYYY)*
13. SIGNATURE OF APPOINTED REPRESENTATIVE, IF ANY (Not required if signed by appellant. See paragraph 6 of the instructions.)	14. DATE *(MM/DD/YYYY)*

This page is followed by a CONTINUATION SHEET FOR ITEM 10.

INFORMATION AND INSTRUCTIONS

Notice from the VA: We are required by law to give you the information in this box. Instructions for filling out the form follow the box.

RESPONDENT BURDEN: VA may not conduct or sponsor, and the respondent is not required to respond to, this collection of information unless it displays a valid Office of Management and Budget (OMB) Control Number. The information requested is approved under OMB Control Number (2900-0085). Public reporting burden for this collection of information is estimated to average one hour per response, including the time for reviewing instructions, searching existing data sources, gathering and maintaining the data needed, and completing and reviewing the collection of information. Send comments regarding this burden estimate or any other aspects of this collection, including suggestions for reducing this burden, to VA Clearance Officer (005E3), 810 Vermont Ave., NW, Washington, DC 20420. DO NOT send requests for benefits to this address.

PRIVACY ACT STATEMENT: Our authority for asking for the information you give to us when you fill out this form is 38 U.S.C. 7105(d)(3), a federal statute that sets out the requirement for you to file a formal appeal to complete your appeal on a VA benefits determination. You use this form to present your appeal to the Board of Veterans' Appeals (BVA). It is used by VA in processing your appeal and it is used by the BVA in deciding your appeal. Providing this information to VA is voluntary, but if you fail to furnish this information VA will close your appeal and you may lose your right to appeal the benefit determinations you told us you disagreed with. The Privacy Act of 1974 (5 U.S.C. 552a) and VA's confidentiality statue (38 U.S.C. 5701), as implemented by 38 CFR 1.526(a) and 1.576(b), require individuals to provide written consent before documents or information can be disclosed to third parties not allowed to receive records or information under any other provision of law. However, the law permits VA to disclose the information you include on this form to people outside of VA in some circumstances. Information about that is given in notices about VA's "systems of records" that are periodically published in the *Federal Register* as required by the Privacy Act of 1974. Examples of situations in which the information included in this form might be released to individuals outside of VA include release to the United States Court of Veterans Appeals, if you later appeal the BVA's decision in your case to that court; disclosure to a medical expert outside of VA, should VA exercise its statutory authority under 38 U.S.C. 5109 or 7109, to ask for an expert medical opinion to help decide your case; disclosure to law enforcement personnel and security guards in order to alert them to the presence of a dangerous person; disclosure to law enforcement agencies should the information indicate that there has been a violation of law; disclosure to a congressional office in order to answer an inquiry from the congressional office made at your request; and disclosure to federal government personnel who have the duty of inspecting VA's records to make sure that they are being properly maintained. See the *Federal Register* notices described above for further details.

INSTRUCTIONS

1. **CONSIDER GETTING ASSISTANCE**: We have tried to give you the general information most people need to complete this form in these instructions, but the law about veterans' benefits can be complicated. If you have a representative, we encourage you to work with your representative in completing this form. If you do not have a representative, we urge you to consider getting one. Most people who appeal to the Board of Veterans' Appeals (BVA) do get a representative. Veterans Service Organizations (VSOs) will represent you at no charge and most people (more than 80 percent) are represented by VSOs. Under certain circumstances, you may pay a lawyer or "agent" to represent you. (See the references in paragraph 9.) Your local VA office can provide you with information about VSOs who are willing to represent you and forms that you will need to complete to appoint either a VSO or an attorney to represent you. Your local bar association may be able to provide you with the names of attorneys who specialize in veterans' law. VA has an 800 number that you can call for assistance: 1-800-827-1000. There are also a few agents recognized by VA who can represent claimants.

2. **WHAT IS THIS FORM FOR?** You told your local VA office that you disagreed with a decision it made on your claim for VA benefits, called filing a "Notice of Disagreement." That office then mailed you a "Statement of the Case" (SOC) that told you why and how it came to the decision that it did. After you have read the SOC, you must decide if you want to go ahead and complete your appeal so that the BVA will review your case. If you do, you or your representative must fill out this form and file it with VA. "Filing" means delivering the completed form to VA in person or by mail. Paragraph 4 tells you how much time you have to file this form and paragraph 7 tells you where you file it. When we refer to "your local VA office" in these instructions, we mean the VA Regional

Office that sent you the "Statement of the Case" or, if you have moved out of the area served by that office, the VA Regional Office that now has your VA records.

3. DO I HAVE TO FILL OUT THIS FORM AND FILE IT? Fill out this form and file it with VA if you want to complete your appeal. If you do not, VA will close your appeal without sending it to the BVA for a decision. If you decide that you no longer want to appeal after you have read the SOC, you don't have to do anything.

4. HOW LONG DO I HAVE TO COMPLETE THIS FORM AND FILE IT? Under current law, there are three different ways to calculate how much time you have to complete and file this form. The one that applies to you is the one that gives you the most time. (a) You have one year from the day your local VA office mailed you the notice of the decision you are appealing. (b) You have sixty days from the day that your local VA office mailed you the SOC. (c) Your local VA office may have sent you an update to the SOC, called a "Supplemental Statement of the Case" (SSOC). Under an opinion by VA's General Counsel, if that SSOC discusses evidence in your case that VA received within the one-year period described in paragraph 4(a) of these instructions, above, and if you have not already filed this form, then you have at least 60 days from the time your local VA office mailed you the SSOC to file it even though the one-year period has already expired.

There is one special kind of case, called a "simultaneously contested claim," where you have thirty days to file this form instead of the longer time periods described above. A "simultaneously contested claim" is a case where two different people are asking for the same kind of VA benefit and one will either lose, or get less, if the other wins. If you are not sure whether this special exception applies, ask your representative or call your local VA office. If you have any questions about the filing deadline in your case, ask your representative or your local VA office. Filing on time is very important. *Failing to file on time could result in you losing your right to appeal.*

5. **WHAT IF I NEED MORE TIME?** If you need more time to complete this form and file it, write to your local VA office, explaining why you need more time. *You must file your request for more time with your local VA office before the normal time for filing this form runs out*. If you file by mail, VA will use the postmark date to decide whether you filed the form, or the request for more time to file it, on time.

6. **WHAT KIND OF INFORMATION DO I NEED TO INCLUDE WHEN I FILL OUT THE FORM?** While most of the form is easy to understand, we will go through the blocks where you might need some additional information.

Block 3. If your appeal involves an insurance claim or some issue related to a VA home loan, enter your VA insurance or VA loan number here. For most kinds of cases, you will leave this block blank.

Blocks 4–7. These blocks are for information about the person who is filing this appeal. If you are a representative filling out this form for the person filing the appeal, fill in the information about that person, not yourself. Block 7 can be left blank if the person filing the appeal is the veteran.

Block 8. It is very important for you to check one, *and only one*, of the boxes in block 8. This lets the VA know whether or not you want an opportunity to appear personally before one or more members of the BVA to give them information about your case, and, if so, where you want to appear. *If you do not check one of the boxes, BVA will assume that you DO NOT want a BVA hearing.*

If you ask for a hearing, you and your representative (if you have one) can present an argument for why you think the BVA should act favorably on your appeal. You can also tell us about the facts behind your claim and you can bring others (witnesses) to the hearing who have information to give the BVA about your case. At your option, you can submit more evidence at a hearing requested on this form. If you do ask for a hearing, it can be very helpful to have a representative assist you at the hearing.

Here is specific information about each of the check boxes in block 8.

Box A: You may feel that you have already sent VA everything the BVA will need to decide your case. It is not necessary for you to have a hearing for BVA to decide your appeal. Check this box if you decide that you do not want a hearing. *If you check this box, do not check any of the other boxes in block 8.*

Boxes B and C: Check box B or box C if you want to appear in person before a member, or members, of the BVA to present your case. We have provided two different boxes because you can have your BVA hearing in one of two different places. You can have your hearing at the BVA's offices in Washington, D.C., or you can ask for a BVA hearing at your local VA office. In making your decision, you should know that VA cannot pay any expenses you (or your representative or witnesses) incur in connection with attending a hearing. Having your BVA hearing at your local VA office is usually less expensive for you because you won't have as much expense for travel for yourself, your witnesses, and your representative. On the other hand, it sometimes takes longer to get your case added to the calendar for BVA hearings at local VA offices because BVA members conduct hearings in the field only during special trips. You can check with your local VA office to get an estimate of how long it may be before your case could be scheduled for a BVA hearing there.

Note: The BVA has initiated a program for conducting hearings electronically. This permits BVA member(s) sitting in Washington, D.C., to hold a hearing with you at your local VA office. Each hears the other through teleconferencing, or hears and sees the other through videoconferencing. We have not provided a check box for this kind of hearing because it is not available at all VA Regional Offices. If you are interested in this kind of hearing, contact your local VA office to see if it is available in your area and inquire about procedures.

HEARINGS BEFORE VA REGIONAL OFFICE PERSONNEL: A hearing before VA Regional Office personnel, instead of before a member of the BVA, is not a BVA hearing. You can request a hearing before VA Regional Office personnel by writing directly to the Regional Office. DO NOT use this form to request that kind of hearing. If you do, it will delay your appeal. You should also know that requesting a hearing before VA Regional Office personnel does not extend the time for filing this form.

Block 9. Save what you want to tell us about *why* you are appealing for the next block. This is the block where you tell us exactly *what* you are appealing. You do this by identifying the "issues" you are appealing. Your local VA office has tried to accurately identify the issues and has listed them on the SOC and any SSOC it sent you. If you think that your local VA office has correctly identified the issues you are appealing and, after reading the SOC and any SSOC you received, you still want to appeal its decisions on all those issues, check the first box in block 9. *Do not check the second box if you check the first box.*

Check the second check box in block 9 if you only want to continue your appeal on some of the issues listed on the SOC and any SSOC you received. List the specific issues you want to appeal in the space under the second box. While you should not use this form to file a new claim or to appeal new issues for the first time, you can also use this space to call the BVA's attention to issues, if any, you told your local VA office in your Notice of Disagreement you wanted to appeal that are not included in the SOC or a SSOC. If you want to file a new claim, or appeal new issues (file a new Notice of Disagreement), do that in separate correspondence.

Block 10. Use this block to tell us why you disagree with the decision made by your local VA office. Tie your arguments to the issues you identified in block 9. Tell us what facts you think VA got wrong and/or how you think VA misapplied the law in your case. Try to be specific. If you are appealing a rating percentage your local VA office assigned for one or more of your service-connected disabilities, tell us *for each service-connected disability rating you have appealed* what rating would satisfy your appeal. (The SOC, or SSOC, includes information about what disability percentages can be assigned for each disability under VA's "Rating Schedule.") You may want to refer to the specific items of evidence that you feel support your appeal, but you do not have to describe all of the evidence you have submitted. The BVA will have your complete file when it considers your case. You should not attach copies of things you have already sent to VA. If you need more space to complete block 10, you can continue it on the back of the form and/or you can attach sheets of paper to the form. If you want to complete this part of the form using a computer word processor, you may do so. Just attach the sheets from your printer to the form and write “see attachment” in block 10.

Block 11. This form can be signed and filed by either the person appealing the local VA decision, or by his or her representative. Sign the form in block 11 if you are the person appealing, or if you are a guardian or other properly appointed fiduciary filing this appeal for someone else. In cases where an incompetent person has no fiduciary, or the fiduciary has not acted, that person's “next friend,” such as a family member, can sign and file this form. If the representative is filing this form, this block can be left blank. Regardless of who signs the form, we encourage you to have your representative check it over before it is filed. Place the date you sign in block 12.

Block 13. If you are a representative filing this form for the appellant, sign here. Otherwise, leave this block blank. If you are an accredited representative of a Veterans Service Organization (VSO), also insert the name of the VSO in this block. Note that signing this form will not serve to appoint you as the appellant's representative. Contact your local VA office if you need information on appointment. Place the date you sign in block 14.

7. WHERE DO I FILE THE FORM ONCE I HAVE COMPLETED IT? When you have completed the form, signed and dated it, send it to the VA office that has your records. Unless you have recently moved outside the area that it serves, this is the office whose address is at the top of the letter VA sent you with the SOC.

8. OTHER SOURCES OF INFORMATION: You can get information about the VA appeals process written in informal language by asking your local VA office for a copy of a pamphlet called “Understanding the Appeal

Process." For more detailed technical information about the VA appeal process, see the BVA's Rules of Practice. You will find them in Part 20 of Title 38 of the Code of Federal Regulations (CFR). Many local public libraries have the CFR, or the library staff may be able to tell you where you can locate a copy. If you have a representative, your representative may have a copy of the CFR. A great deal of information is available on the Internet at "http://www.va.gov." (Do not include the quotation marks or the final period when typing in the Internet address.)

9. SPECIAL NOTE FOR ATTORNEYS AND VA ACCREDITED AGENTS. There are statutory and regulatory restrictions on the payment of your fees and expenses and requirements for filing copies of your fee agreement with your client with VA. See 38 U.S.C. 5904 and 38 CFR 20.609-.610.

ACKNOWLEDGMENTS

I owe a debt of appreciation to some very special people who volunteered their time and ideas to help me focus on the best methods with which to advise veterans on how to fight the VA in the trenches and make it count. First, let me say thank you to Robert Tralins, a fiction writer of action stories, with more than 250 covers notched on his pen, who always offered another idea to consider. Bob and I went to the mats with our fight for his VA benefits. We won.

To Dr. Susan Demers, LLB, Program Director, *Legal Assisting*, St. Petersburg College, Florida, who has an endless list of kudos as teacher of future litigators and advocates, as past president of the Clearwater Bar Association, and a commissioner on the Florida Bar President's Special Commission on Paralegal Regulations. My thirst to go for the jugular started when I enrolled in her program. Thanks Susan for all of your fantastic ideas.

Finally, thank you to Attorney John E. Tuthill, who I met when we were defending the rights of the same veteran. I was impressed with his passion to help veterans. His practice in St. Petersburg, Florida, deals with family, criminal, military, and veterans law. John is a retired captain, U.S. Navy JAG Corps, who served thirty-three years and was one of the navy's first two reserve appellate judges serving in Washington, D.C. He was twice awarded the prestigious Pinellas County Victim Rights Coalition award.

To my wife of more than five decades, Patsy, I send love and bouquets forever. Thank you for always being willing to read my manuscripts and tell me when I get off course.

INTRODUCTION: READ ME FIRST

You have elected to appeal the denial of service connection for an injury or illnesses that was incurred while you were in the service. The grounds for your appeal are that you are dissatisfied by the decision that the VA handed down after you filed a claim.

FAQ: What are the most common reasons for veterans to appeal claims?

Veterans appeal their claims when the VA has denied them benefits for a disability they believe began in the service and when they believe their disability is more severe than the VA rated it.

FAQ: What do I do first once I have decided to appeal the VA's decision?

Now that you have chosen to appeal the denial of your claim for disability benefits, first you must accept that this challenge to the VA's decision to deny you service connection for your injury or illness will more than likely take several years to resolve. Second, you must accept that you and you alone are responsible for proving your claim. Like any project you attempt, you have to start at the beginning and then work toward a solution step by step. The following section, titled "The Appeals Process: Step by Step," will walk you through the various stages you will go through when appealing your claim.

FAQ: Was my claim denied because of something I did wrong or because of the VA?

You are where you are for one of two reasons: you were responsible for your claim being denied or the VA was responsible. It could also be a combination of errors by both groups. Part 1 of *Claim Denied* points out the most common mistakes veterans make when applying for service-connected benefits, such as failure to provide evidence to suport a claim, failure to prepare the appropriate forms, failure to follow up on documents you may have submitted. These issues, among others, will be covered thoroughly and will be accompanied by practical tips that you may follow to increase your chances of successfully appealing your claim. Part 2 of *Claim Denied* addresses the possible errors the VA committed when appealing your claim.

FAQ: How do I know what to do to successfully claim benefits?

This book's purpose is to help you defend your claim for benefits. Only provable facts will win your appeal. Your arguments must be in a format that is well organized and logical to the reviewing authority. The basics are easy to understand but you have to know them. Appealing a VA decision is not impossible.

THE APPEALS PROCESS:
STEP BY STEP

THE SUBSTANTIVE APPEAL

You have the right to appeal your claim!

Veterans Affairs would like you to believe that appealing a decision is nothing more than submitting the VA Form 9 Substantive Appeal, which briefly states the reasons why you are refuting the VA's decision. Accepting this premise will guarantee a two- to three-year wait for the Board of Veterans' Appeals (BVA) to rule on your appeal. The odds are against BVA affirming your appeal.

However, the VA can be successfully challenged. To do so you must know the basics:

- The VA often sends out letters that are confusing to the veteran.
- Very seldom will a veteran have copies of all the evidence in his or her claim file.
- Compensation and Pension Examinations (C&Ps) are often flawed.

- A Statement of the Case contains only the VA's interpretation of the evidence.

- Most claims are decided by an individual rater rather than by more than one adjudicator.

- Many times a VA decision is based on conjecture rather than on hard evidence.

- Rating Officers do not have the professional medical and legal backgrounds necessary to understand the complexities of rating the residuals of an injury or illness.

- Rating Officers and Decision Review Officers often fail to follow prescribed protocol when deciding a claim.

- Adjudicators tend to disregard statements from lay persons or the appellant when deciding the claim.

- Adjudicators often disregard circumstantial evidence supporting a veteran's claim.

- The U.S. Court of Appeals for Veterans Claims (CAVC) has shown that the VA has demanded the burden of proof from the veteran, which exceeds the intent of the law.

Remember, the VA is a bureaucracy:

. . . a large, complex administrative structure. These structures exist in organizations such as governments and businesses with a hierarchy of bureaus and agencies.

. . . a formal organization with defined objectives, a hierarchy of specialized roles and systematic processes of direction and administration.

. . . a system in which people are expected to follow precisely defined rules and procedures rather than to use personal judgment.

The most important thing is to not quit in frustration.

STEPS OF THE APPEALS PROCESS

Claim filed ⇨

Claim decided (denied) ⇨

Veteran disagrees with the decision ⇨

Notice of Disagreement submitted ⇨

Statement of the Case is issued ⇨

Substantive Appeal completed ⇨

Veteran requests a hearing ⇨

Hearing with Board of Veterans' Appeals conducted ⇨

Decision made ●

WHY THESE EXAMPLES ARE IMPORTANT

Examples are provided for you so that you can present your appeal arguments in complete harmony with the statutes, regulations, and case laws. Framing your appeal based on the supportive second-tier level of evidence will warrant granting service connection for the disability or disabilities claimed. No matter how well supported and organized your presentation, Regional Office adjudicators are known to ignore your arguments and let the Board of Veterans' Appeals decide the merits of the appeal.

Keep in mind that for the VA to prevail it must produce medical evidence, other than the department's unsubstantiated opinion, from an outside source that reflects a preponderance of evidence against your claim. Further, the VA must be able to explain exactly why its evidence negates the evidence you have furnished.

Going Forward

You have already made the most important decision: to appeal the denial of your claim for disability benefits. Now a thousand questions go racing through your mind:

What is the VA talking about in my claim denial?
What do they mean I have a year to file an appeal?
What do I have to do to make them grant the benefit?
How long will this appeal process take?
Can I make them speed up my appeal?
How do I prove their decision is wrong?
How do I know they rated my claim fairly?

Why didn't they believe me the first time?
Didn't they get the proof and evidence I told them about?
How do I find the type of evidence they will accept as proof positive?
How do I find military records to support the claim that I was injured in the service?
Can I successfully rebut their decision to deny benefits?
How do I know if they will really help me?
Who can help me if they don't?

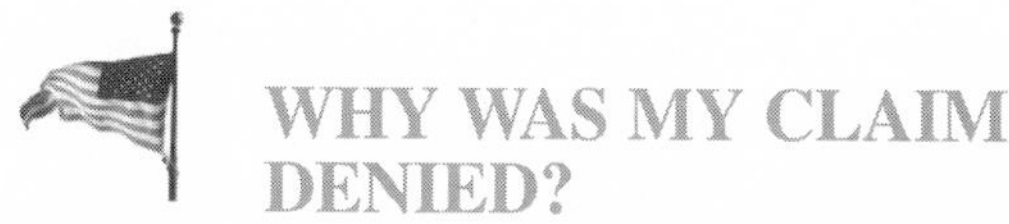

WHY WAS MY CLAIM DENIED?

Before covering the basic categories of appeals—New Claims Appeal, New and Material Evidence Appeal, and Clear and Unmistakable Error Appeal—we need to take a look at the overall basics of the appeal process.

When appealing a decision made by the VA, there are two forms that must be used: VA Form 21-4138 Statement in Support of Claim and VA Form 9 Appeal to Board of Veterans' Appeals. To begin the appeal process, file a Notice of Disagreement using VA Form 21-4138 with the Regional Office that processed your claim. This is a notice to the VA that you do not accept its decision to deny entitlement or the amount of entitlement for compensation benefits.

This notice should be a very simple statement saying you do not agree with the decision.

At this point, do not give the reasons why you disagree.

The VA will respond with a Statement of the Case (SOC).

The next stage in the appeal process is filing a Substantive Appeal, which is submitted on VA Form 9. You have one year from the day your local VA office mails you the notice of its decision to effect your appeal.[1] Preparation of a formal appeal requires considerable organization, research, and documentation showing why the Board of Veterans' Appeals should reverse the Regional Office's denial of benefits. At this time, you should ask for a hearing before the Board of Veterans' Appeals. If the BVA upholds the Regional Office's decision you can petition the BVA for reconsideration.

Local VA offices will send a Supplemental Statement of the Case (SSOC) if, after reviewing the additional evidence submitted, it maintains that you are not entitled to benefits or if the VA complies with the remand order from the BVA and maintains you are not entitled to benefits.

Under an opinion by the VA's General Counsel, if an SSOC is sent to you and the one-year grace period has expired, you are still entitled to rebut their reasons if you submit your arguments within sixty days from the date of the SSOC. To ensure you are in compliance with the suspense date, always send your response by certified mail with a request for return receipt. This way, if you are close to the deadline, you can prove your response was postmarked prior to the expiration of the sixty-day or one-year date.

Next, file a formal appeal on VA Form 9 Appeal to

---

1. Service connection may be granted on a presumptive basis under 38 CFR 3.307 if this condition is manifested to a compensable degree (severe enough to be evaluated at least 10 percent disabling) within one year after military discharge.

Board of Veterans' Appeals. If this effort fails, you can file an appeal with the U.S. Court of Appeals for Veterans Claims.

TYPES OF APPEALS

You must choose between two types of appeals based either on new and material evidence or on a clear and unmistakable error. The type of claim you are appealing will determine how you should proceed.

New and Material Evidence Appeal

Submitting new and material evidence is a way to revisit a previously denied claim. The New and Material Evidence Appeal argues that new medical evidence and documents submitted for the purpose of reopening a previously denied claim are relevant. When the VA denies a claim for disability benefits, you have one year from the date of the denial letter to challenge the VA's decision. Once that date has expired, you cannot reverse the denial of benefits unless you can submit new and material evidence or find a clear and unmistakable error. The new and material evidence cannot be evidence that is already on record or merely cumulative of other evidence in the record.

What Qualifies as New and Material Evidence?

The VA defines new and material evidence for the adjudicator in VA Regulation 38 CFR §3.156 (a), which states the following:

> New evidence means existing evidence not previously

> submitted to agency decision makers. Material evidence means existing evidence that, by itself or when considered with previous evidence of record, relates to an unestablished fact necessary to substantiate the claim. New and material evidence can be neither cumulative nor redundant of the evidence of record at the time of the last prior final denial of the claim sought to be reopened, and must raise a reasonable possibility of substantiating the claim.[2]

If you intend to reopen a denied claim, reread all correspondence from the VA before taking any action. You should substitute the facts of your case for those in the *Justine Branch v. Togo D. West, Jr.* case. During the process of rereading the court's explanation of its decision, ask yourself the following questions: Do I see why the Court said the medical evidence was new? Am I now disabled because of the military injury or illness? Do I understand what "probative" means in the context of material?

Many veterans submit a lay statement from a former buddy attesting to medical circumstances as new material and evidence. This is not acceptable because your buddy is not necessarily a medical professional.

An appeal pending before the Board of Veterans' Ap-

---

2. To understand the meaning of "New and Material" you may wish to read the following Court cases on the subject: *Lois K. Embry, Appellant, v. Togo D. West, Jr. Secretary of Veterans Affairs, Appellee*, before IVERS, Associate Judge Docket No. 99-70, A MEMORANDUM DECISION; and *Harlow Forrest, Appellant, v. Jesse Brown, Secretary of Veterans Affairs, Appellee*, before STEINBERG, Associate Judge. Docket No. 90-' 29', A MEMORANDUM DECISION.

peals is not usually reviewed for several years. If the BVA agrees that the evidence is new and material, the claim will be returned to the Regional Office of original jurisdiction to be readjudicated.

VA Rating Teams have enormous discretionary power to interpret evidence submitted in a new claim action to reopen a previously denied claim. The Rating Team determines if the new evidence meets the criteria based on the Rating Team's overall experience in applying the guidelines outlined in VA regulations, manuals, and case law as well as understanding the medical issues involved and how the new evidence relates to the medical facts already in the record. Adjudicators may have no more knowledge of what constitutes new and material evidence than you do, but if they have the slightest doubt as to the merits of your arguments they will err on the side of the government. If the VA decides, after considering all the evidence, that your illness or injury is not service-related, you have to start the appeal process over again. Thus it is beneficial to take your time and submit a thoroughly researched appeal.

To attain a better understanding of what constitutes new and material evidence, go to the U.S. Court of Appeals for Veterans Claims website. Click on Decisions and Opinions, then click ISYS System Search, and last, search for New and Material Evidence. The U.S. Court of Appeals for Veterans Claims has visited this issue more than four thousand times since 1990. This shows there is a great deal of controversy in interpreting what constitutes new evidence that is material to an appeal. Reading cases that the Court did not approve can be very helpful, for they will show you what the veteran failed to do, which will help you avoid similar mistakes.

CASE LAW: *BRANCH V. WEST*

To illustrate the complexities of an appeal based on new and material evidence, U.S. Court of Appeals for Veterans Claims Docket No. 97-1675, *Justine Branch v. Togo D. West, Jr., Secretary of Veterans Affairs* shows the Court's rationale, which may help you to understand what you must consider and do for a successful appeal.

In a final decision, dated February 18, 1964, the Board of Veterans' Appeals denied the veteran, Branch, service connection for chest pains and headaches. The Board stated that the headaches and chest pains were "not substantiated by the manifestation of any disease entity or disability during service, at discharge there from or subsequent thereto." Evidence submitted since that decision includes: (1) an application for compensation or pension for headaches and chest pains, received in June 1994; (2) private medical records dated from 1983 to 1988 showing treatment for high blood pressure; (3) private medical records dated from 1988 to 1994 showing treatment for high blood pressure, headaches, and lower back pain and showing a diagnosis of "costochondral of chest"; and (4) a statement in support of the claim, submitted in October 1994, in which Branch states that during service he had been frequently beaten in the stomach, chest, and head and that he has experienced chest pains and headaches continuously since that time.

In January 1995, a VA regional office determined that new and material evidence had not been presented to reopen the claims for service connection for headaches and chest pains. Branch filed a Notice of Disagreement (NOD); a Statement of the Case was issued; and the appellant then filed a Substantive Appeal. In the decision on appeal, the Board initially determined that the medical evidence presented since the February 1964 board decision was new. The Board further concluded that the evidence was not material because, in the absence of medical evidence relating a current disability owing to headaches or chest pains to service, there was no reasonable possibility of outcome change.

With regard to the claim for service connection for a disability owing to chest pains, the evidence submitted since the last final disallowance is new because it is not "merely cumulative" of other evidence in the record, and it is probative as to the bases for the last final disallowance because it provides lay evidence of an in-service incurrence and medical evidence of a current disability. However, because Branch did not provide medical evidence of a nexus between his current disability owing to chest pains and his service, there is no reasonable possibility that the claim will be granted. Establishing service connection generally requires medical evidence of a current disability or, in certain circumstances, lay evidence of in-service incurrence or aggravation of a disease or injury and medical evidence of nexus between the claimed in-service disease or injury and the present disease or injury.

Lay statements of causation are not sufficient to

continued on next page

continued from previous page

meet the medical nexus requirement. In view of the foregoing, the Court held that new and material evidence had not been presented to reopen the disallowed claim for service connection for chest pains.

"With regard to the claim for service connection for a disability due to headaches, the evidence submitted since the last final disallowance is new, and it is probative because it provides lay evidence of an in-service incurrence. The record, however, is devoid of any medical evidence of a current disability due to headaches or medical evidence of a nexus between such a current disability and service. Even assuming that the appellant's lay statements would be sufficient to show a current disability due to headaches, there is, in the absence of medical nexus evidence, no reasonable possibility of outcome change. Consequently, the Court holds that new and material evidence also has not been presented to reopen the disallowed claim for service connection for a disability due to headaches."[3]

This case shows the importance of understanding what qualifies as new and material evidence and substantiating your claim, which requires proving all four elements. The case also shows a missed opportunity: the veteran failed to reopen his claim when he was diagnosed with costochondral of the chest, which is

---

3. See U.S. Court of Appeals for Veterans Claims, Docket No. 97-1675, *Justine Branch v. Togo D. West, Jr., Secretary of Veterans Affairs*. To see this decision in its entirety go to http://search.vetapp.gov/search/. Type in the search box "New and Material Evidence" and click on the search button. Then click on docket number 96-1675.

often the result of injuries caused by being repeatedly beaten in the stomach, chest, and head. He should have explored the possibility by having his physician write a report pointing out that such trauma would more than likely produce the veteran's current symptoms. The medical specialist should have also included a reference that this type of injury may not manifest itself to generate pain symptoms for many years after the repeated traumas to the body have stopped.

Background research on traumatic brain injury (TBI) itself would have uncovered facts, published by the U.S. Center for Disease Control (CDC), that could have proved repeated beating to the head to be responsible for the veteran's headaches. The CDC published facts that claim that repeated mild TBI occurring over an extended period of time (months or years) can result in cumulative neurological and cognitive deficit, for "[a TBI] is caused by a blow or jolt to the head or a penetrating head injury that disrupts the function of the brain."

The veteran also needed to establish he was beaten while on active duty, which is difficult to prove, but not impossible. And a final factor that weakened this veteran's case was inconsistent medical records. The earliest medical records introduced in the case were dated approximately twenty years after he was denied benefits in 1964. Furthermore, there were no medical records between 1983 and 1994 related to his initial claim for chest pains and headaches. Failing to tie together all these records would lead any Ratings Team to question a claim's legitimacy.

continued on next page

continued from previous page

To successfully challenge a VA decision to deny benefits, you must back up every statement of fact with tangible evidence. Merely saying one was frequently beaten counts for nothing if there is no proof. To put together a case thirty years after the fact is a long shot at best. What Branch needed was an adviser who knew how to take a cold case and run with it. Sadly, there are very few advocates who can offer that type of counseling and assistance to veterans. However, now that attorneys are allowed to defend a veteran's claim immediately after it is denied, veterans' chances of winning an appeal are greatly improved. ●

Regulation Definition of New and Material Evidence

If the service department sends additional records before or after a decision becomes final, the Ratings Team must rerate the claim considering this new evidence. 38 CFR §3.156(c) exists for the protection of veterans, ensuring their claim is given every consideration. Very few veteran Service Officers or veterans think to make sure the Ratings Team complies with the regulation. If you evaluate the evidence on record and come across documents in your file that establish that the service department sent records to the Regional Office after the Regional Office decided your claim and the Regional Office took no action on this evidence, you have a winning hand, even if your original claim was dated 1962. The regulation states in part:

> Where the new and material evidence consists of a supplemental report from the service department, received before or after the decision has become final, the former decision will be reconsidered by the adjudicating agency of original jurisdiction. This comprehends official service department records that presumably have been misplaced and have now been located and forwarded to the Department of Veterans Affairs. Also included are corrections by the service department of former errors of commission or omission in the preparation of the prior report or reports and identified as such. The retroactive evaluation of disability resulting from disease or injury subsequently service-connected on the bases of the new evidence from the service department must be supported adequately by medical evidence. Where such records clearly support the assignment of a specific rating over a part or the entire period of time involved, a retroactive evaluation will be assigned accordingly except as it may be affected by the filing date of the original claim.

This is important information should you locate copies of original active duty records that directly relate to your claim. Sometimes records that were supposedly lost or destroyed can be attained through a request for the missing records under the Freedom of Information Act (FOIA).

There are several possible reasons the VA may not turn over documents immediately. First, the request from the VA could have been accidentally lost somewhere in the internal mail system at the National Personnel Record Center–Military Personnel Records (NPRC-MPR) and the VA may not have followed up on its request but simply dispatched a letter saying it was advised that the records were destroyed in the 1973 fire at NPRC-MPR. Second, an NPRC-MPR clerk may have overlooked the records and assumed they were destroyed in the fire. Third, the records could have been misfiled initially and at a later date the error was discovered and the records were correctly filed. Because there was no current request for these records, they were simply put in storage. Instead of taking anything for granted, check and recheck the status of every piece of evidence needed to support your claim.

Clear and Unmistakable Error Appeal

A clear and unmistakable error can be established only when three conditions are not met. First, the correct facts in the record were not put before the adjudicator, or the statutory or regulatory provisions in existence at the time were applied incorrectly. Second, the alleged error must be indisputable, not merely a disagreement, as to how the facts were weighed or evaluated. Third, the commission of the alleged error must have manifestly changed the outcome of the decision being appealed on the basis of clear and unmistakable error at the time that decision was rendered. The veteran's allegation of clear and unmistakable error must identify alleged errors specifically and give persuasive reasons as to why the result would have been manifestly different.

Appealing a case based on clear and unmistakable error is much tougher than appealing based on new and material evidence. The CAVC and the Board of Veterans' Appeals are very strict with their definition of what is a clear and unmistakable error. The Clear and Unmistakable Error Appeal has been before the U.S. Court of Appeals for Veterans Claims 1,603 times since 1989, of which 335 cases were decided by a panel of three judges.

How Do I Make a Clear and Unmistakable Error Appeal?

If you decide to make a Clear and Unmistakable Error Appeal, it would be beneficial to seek out an expert in the field. You can win this type of appeal, but it depends on you or your advocate's ability to acquire all the facts and prepare the arguments for your case based on regulations and statutes that were enforced at the time of the alleged error.

First, obtain a copy of your complete claim file. If you were treated in a VA hospital or clinic, you must request these records from those institutions. VA medical treatment records are not forwarded to the Regional Office routinely unless the Regional Office has specifically requested them. If one or more VA Medical Center or clinic has treated you, each source must be contacted individually. You must explore every possible source for evidence that will substantiate your case.

LETTER OF DENIAL

Take a good look at the example letter (pp. 20–21) and see what it is telling you. Note that the decision date is *November 18, 2007,* making November 18, 2008, the fail-safe date to rebut the denial of benefits. The date, April 2, 2007, is the date the VA acknowledged acceptance of your claim. When the appeal is reversed, the date the VA officially accepted your claim will be your entitlement date. Also, the statutes spell out that the benefit payment date is the first day of the month following the month the claim was filed. Since the date stamped here is April 2, 2007, the retroactive payment date will be adjusted to May 1, 2007.

Your next action is to determine what disability was denied. Make certain that the VA identifies the disability you claimed. In the example, the veteran filed his claim for coronary artery disease (CAD), with anxiety and depression secondary to CAD. If you filed a claim for several disabilities, make sure that they are all addressed. If you don't follow up on a disability that is missing on the list, the VA will assume you are in agreement with its decision in its entirety.

Example of Letter of Denial of Benefits

JAMES R. ROGERS
4500 IAMVET STREET
WASHINGTON, DC 20420

In Reply Refer To:
P 317/VSC/ OST4/tes
C 122-22-5555
ROGERS, JAMES R.

November 18, 2007

Dear Mr. Rogers:

We made a decision on your claim for service-connected compensation received on April 2, 2007.

This letter tells you what we decided. It includes a copy of our rating decision that gives the evidence used and reasons for our decision. We have also included information about what to do if you disagree with our decision, and who to contact if you have questions or need assistance.

What Did We Decide?

We determined that the following conditions were not related to your military service, so service connection couldn't be granted:

Medical Description
Coronary artery disease adjustment disorder with anxiety and depressed mood

Your compensation payment will continue unchanged at $917.00, 60% service connection.

We have enclosed a copy of your rating decision for your review. It provides a detailed explanation of our decision, the evidence considered and the reasons for our decision. You can find the decision discussed in the section titled *"Decision."* The evidence we considered is discussed in the section titled *"Evidence."* The reasons for our decision can be found in the portion of the rating titled *"Reasons for Decision"* or *"Reasons and Bases."*

What You Should Do If You Disagree with Our Decision

If you do not agree with our decision, you should write and tell us why. You have *one year from the date of this letter to appeal the decision.* The enclosed *VA form 4107 Your Rights to Appeal Our Decision* explains your right to appeal.

Request Copies of VA Records

Next, citing the Freedom of Information Act as your authority, send a VA Form 21-4138 to each VA hospital or VA clinic that may have hospital or medical treatment records on you concerning all injuries or illnesses. Make certain you specifically request a copy of the Compensation and Pension Examination and any special test that might have been scheduled. You will see in Part 3 why this information is critical and why entitlement might hinge on the fact that you are aware of the results from these tests. These records are not only important for establishing entitlement, but they can also help you determine if you were rated properly in accordance with 38 CFR Part 4. If you were already in receipt of compensation benefits for another disability, the VA will comment on the current status of that entitlement. Two important actions will take place at this point. First, the previously granted disability may have been reevaluated and the VA may have concluded your existing service-connected disability has improved, which will then reduce or terminate this benefit. A previously granted disability becomes untouchable only if it has been enforced for twenty or more years.

Second, if the VA takes no action against the existing benefits, your current disabilities will be continued at the current rate. For example, the VA communicated to the veteran in the letter that his current benefits would be continued at the current rate of $960 per month. The VA finally closes out the letter by stating that a copy of the rating decision and the reason or reasons why the claim was denied is attached.

Start Researching

While you are waiting for these documents to be sent to you, start gathering facts about your injury or illness to support your appeal. Find out the cause of your injury or illness, if it is exacerbated by stress, your environment, or other factors, what symptoms do you have as a result, if these symptoms are progressive, if other kinds of factors, injuries, or diseases will feed or accelerate your current condition, etc. Veteran Rogers, in the example, to his surprise, found that high-stress jobs, continuous exposure to high-decibel sounds, gum disease, shift work, high-fat military diets, and long, irregular hours played a role in the development of CAD. As he explored these categories, he printed copies of the medical findings to submit along with his appeal. When you nail down answers relevant to your own questions, make certain you print copies of this information.

Websites run by government health agencies, universities, medical schools, and libraries; the American Medical Association's monthly publications *JAMA* and *Archives Journal*; and studies published by VA medical researchers usually contain this information.

A NEW CLAIM APPEAL

There are eleven types of claims that the VA considers a new claim:

Original Claim whereby the veteran applies for compensation benefits based on injuries or illnesses for which he has never previously filed.

Claim for Increased Benefits is an action whereby the veteran alleges his or her service-connected medical problem has become more disabling, thus requiring more compensation.

Amending an Original Claim whereby the veteran alleges that another medical problem never previously claimed is also service-related.

Total Disability Based on Individual Unemployability Claim arises when the veteran alleges that his service-connected disability or disabilities make him unemployable.

Special Compensation Claim is an action whereby the veteran has alleged that the service-related medical problem or problems entitle him to a rating greater than 100 percent.

Post-traumatic Stress Disorder Claim is an action that is founded on the basis of the veteran's combat experiences that result in mental health issues.

Claim Based on Medical Treatment by the VA is an action whereby the veteran alleges a permanent disability is the result of the medical treatment he received at a VA medical facility.

Adjunct Disabilities Claim occurs when the veteran alleges his service-connected injury or illness caused another medical disability.

Presumptive Diseases Claim alleges that the veteran's medical issues are considered to be presumptive in accordance with 38 CFR §3.309(a)(b) or (3).

Pension Claim is applicable when a wartime veteran alleges his nonservice injury or illness makes him unemployable and what income he has is below the national income poverty level.

Burial Benefits Claim is an action by the heirs of a veteran alleging there is entitlement to a burial allowance because the veteran's death was a result of a service-related injury or illness.

The first action that must be taken once you have established the time frame you have to effect your appeal is the immediate request for copies of all records maintained by the VA Regional Office. As you will note from the text of the request, you are asking for everything they have about you.

Next, citing the Freedom of Information Act, send a VA Form 21-4138 to each VA hospital or VA clinic that may have your hospital or medical treatment records. Make certain you specifically request a copy of the Compensation and Pension Examination and any special test that might have been scheduled. Entitlement may hinge on the fact that you are aware of the results of these tests. These records are not only important for establishing entitlement, but they can also help you determine if you were rated properly in accordance with 38 CFR Part 4.

You cannot successfully challenge the VA unless you know on what evidence and records they have based their decisions. It is your responsibility to prove if they have erred. To ensure the request does not get lost in the system, have your congressional representative submit it for you. Remember, any information that flows through your congressional representative's office to the VA must be quickly processed. The VA will acknowledge receipt of your request to the congressional representative, and when the files are all copied, the VA will advise your representative that a copy of your file has been shipped to you.

NOTICE OF DISAGREEMENT

Your records have now arrived from the VA—you are ready to take the next step in the appeals process: preparing your Notice of Disagreement. Before you begin, screen all the documents and records the VA sent and compare them to what the Ratings Officer stated in the rating decision. Did the Ratings Officer in fact identify and address all the evidence that was favorable to your claim? If you find the slightest infraction of a statute, regulation, or case law, which is binding on the raters or on the Board of

Typical Request for Claim File Records
(VA Form 21-4138)

STATEMENT IN SUPPORT OF CLAIM

PRIVACY ACT INFORMATION: The VA will not disclose information collected on this form to any source other than what has been authorized under the Privacy Act of 1974 or Title 38, Code of Federal Regulations 1.576 for routine uses (i.e., civil or criminal law enforcement, congressional communications, epidemiological or research studies, the collection of money owed to the United States, litigation in which the United States is a party or has an interest, the administration of VA Programs and delivery of VA benefits, verification of identity and status, and personnel administration) as identified in the VA system of records, 58VA21/22, Compensation, Pension, Education and Rehabilitation Record–VA, published in the *Federal Register*. Your obligation to respond is required to obtain or retain benefits. VA uses your SSN to identify your claim file. Providing your SSN will help ensure that your records are properly associated with your claim file.

FIRST NAME **JAMES** MIDDLE **R** *(Type or print)* **James R. Rogers**	LAST **ROGERS**	VA FILE NO. C/CSS **112-22-5555** SOCIAL SECURITY NO. **112-22-5555**

The following statement is made in connection with a claim for benefits in the case of the above-named veteran:

Under the provisions of the Freedom of Information Act I request a complete copy of all documents and records to include any inter-team memos, C&P Examination requests and responses thereto, military medical and nonmedical records, copies of all letters sent

by VA on my behalf to agencies of the government and non-government sources and the response from said requests.

I CERTIFY THAT the statements on this form are true and correct to the best of my knowledge and belief.

SIGNATURE
James R. Rogers

DATE SIGNED
November 20, 2007

ADDRESS
4500 IAMVET STREET
WASHINGTON, DC 20420

TELEPHONE NUMBERS
(Include Area Code)
DAYTIME **700-555-0000**
EVENING **Same**

Typical Request for VA Medical Records

STATEMENT IN SUPPORT OF CLAIM

PRIVACY ACT INFORMATION: The VA will not disclose information collected on this form to any source other than what has been authorized under the Privacy Act of 1974 or Title 38, Code of Federal Regulations 1.576 for routine uses (i.e., civil or criminal law enforcement, congressional communications, epidemiological or research studies, the collection of money owed to the United States, litigation in which the United States is a party or has an interest, the administration of VA Programs and delivery of VA benefits, verification of identity and status, and personnel administration) as identified in the VA system of records, 58VA21/22, Compensation, Pension, Education and Rehabilitation Record–VA, published in the *Federal Register*. Your obligation to respond is required to obtain or retain benefits. VA uses your SSN to identify your claim file. Providing your SSN will help ensure that your records are properly associated with your claim file.

continued on next page

continued from previous page

FIRST NAME **JAMES**	MIDDLE **R**	LAST **ROGERS**	VA FILE NO. C/CSS **112-22-5555**
(Type or print) **James R. Rogers**			SOCIAL SECURITY NO. **112-22-5555**

The following statement is made in connection with a claim for benefits in the case of the above-named veteran:

Under the provisions of the Freedom of Information Act I request a complete copy of my C&P Examination and the results from all ordered tests as well as the comments by the chief of the C&P Division. I further request a copy of all treatment records at XYZ, VA Medical Center, and VA Clinic in Washington, D.C. My examination was conducted on June 5, 2005. I also request copies of all in-patient and outpatient treatment records. This would include doctor notes, nursing notes, laboratory test results and discharge summary.

I CERTIFY THAT the statements on this form are true and correct to the best of my knowledge and belief.

SIGNATURE	DATE SIGNED
James R. Rogers	**November 20, 2007**

ADDRESS	TELEPHONE NUMBERS *(Include Area Code)*
4500 IAMVET STREET	DAYTIME **700-555-0000**
WASHINGTON, DC 20420	EVENING **Same**

Typical Request for Military Records
from NPRC

Standard Form 180 (Rev. 4-07) (Page I)
Prescribed by NARA (36 CFR 1228.168(b))

Authorized for local reproduction
Previous edition unusable

OMB No. 3095-0029 Expires 9/30/2008
To ensure the next possible service, please thoroughly review the accompanying instructions before filling out this form. Please print clearly or type. If you need more space, use plain paper

REQUEST PERTAINING TO MILITARY RECORDS

SECTION I—INFORMATION NEEDED TO LOCATE RECORDS

(Furnish as much as possible.)

1. NAME USED DURING SERVICE (last, first, and middle)

Rogers, James R.

2. SOCIAL SECURITY NO.
112-22-5555
3. DATE OF BIRTH
04-15-1950
4. PLACE OF BIRTH
Baltimore, MD

5. SERVICE, PAST AND PRESENT
(For an effective records search, it is important that all service be shown below.)

BRANCH OF SERVICE		DATES OF SERVICE: DATE ENTERED	DATES OF SERVICE: DATE RELEASED	CHECK ONE: OFFICER/	CHECK ONE: ENLISTED	SERVICE NUMBER DURING THIS PERIOD (If unknown, write "unknown")
a. ACTIVE SERVICE	USAF	04-15-1971	04-30-1991	X		112-22-5555
b. RESERVE SERVICE	USMCR	04-15-1967	04-01-1971		X	112-22-5555
c. NATIONAL GUARD						

6. IS THIS PERSON DECEASED? If "YES" enter the date of death.
☒ NO ☐ YES

7. IS (WAS) THIS PERSON RETIRED FROM MILITARY SERVICE?
☐ NO ☒ YES

continued on next page

continued from previous page

SECTION II — INFORMATION AND/OR DOCUMENTS REQUESTED

1. REPORT OF SEPARATION (DD Form 214 or equivalent). This contains information normally needed to verify military service. A copy may be sent to the veteran, the deceased veteran's next of kin, or other persons or organizations if authorized in Section III, below. NOTE: If more than one period of service was performed, even in the same branch, there may be more than one Report of Separation. Be sure to show EACH year that a Report of Separation was issued, for which you need a copy.

☒ An UNDELETED Report of Separation is requested for the year(s) **1971, 1991**

This normally will be a copy of the full separation document including such sensitive items as the character of separation, authority for separation, reason for separation, reenlistment eligibility code, separation (SPD/SPN) code, and dates of time lost. An undeleted version is ordinarily required to determine eligibility for benefits.

☐ A DELETED Report of Separation is requested for the year(s)

The following information will be deleted from the copy sent: authority for separation, reason for separation, reenlistment eligibility code, separation (SPD/SPN) code, and for separations after June 30, 1979, character of separation and dates of time lost.

2. OTHER INFORMATION AND/OR DOCUMENTS REQUESTED
Awards and Declaration to include citations, MOS & AFSC, all active duty records to include copies of assignment orders, LODs, TDY records, and overseas assignment orders

3. PURPOSE (Optional — An explanation of the purpose of the request is strictly voluntary. Such information may help the agency answering this request to provide the best possible response and will in no way be used to make a decision to deny the request.) **To support my claim for VA disability benefits based on combat and noncombat injuries**

SECTION III—RETURN ADDRESS AND SIGNATURE

REQUESTER IS:

☒ Military service member or veteran identified in Section I, above

☐ Legal guardian (must submit copy of court appointment)

☐ Next of kin of deceased veteran ☐ Other (specify relation)

SEND INFORMATION/DOCUMENTS TO:

James R. Rogers, 1600 IAmVet Drive, Washington, DC 21250

Veterans' Appeals, you are on the road to reversing the Ratings Officer's decision.

An important tip: identify everything in the rating decision you disagree with. For example, if you filed a claim with five issues, make sure to address all five in your Notice of Disagreement. The VA will assume that you are in agreement with their decision on the fifth issue if you identify only four. The legal interpretation of failing to identify an issue is known as "failure to perfect your appeal." Failure to address all the issues could cost you health benefits and compensation.

The Notice of Disagreement is a notice to the VA that you do not accept its decision to deny entitlement or the amount of entitlement for compensation benefits. This notice should be a simple statement saying you do not agree with the decision. At this point, do not list the reasons you disagree; you will give your reasons for disagreement when you file your formal appeal, VA Form 9 Substantive Appeal. Whenever possible, use VA Form 21-4138 rather than on your own stationery.

STATEMENT OF THE CASE

With a written receipt of your Notice of Disagreement, the VA will send a Statement of the Case, which describes what facts, laws, and regulations were used in deciding the case. This document is simply the VA's interpretation and justification of its denial of your service-connected benefits. Before we move on to the mechanics of preparing an appeal, you should know what the VA's responsibilities include when preparing a Statement of the Case, especially its duty to furnish the Statement of the Case in a timely manner. Failure to do so may be considered a denial of due process, which is the idea that the law and government must provide fair procedures.

The Date

All actions pivot on the date. On the first page of the cover letter accompanying the Statement of the Case, the VA states, "You must file your appeal with this office within sixty days from the date of this letter or within the remainder, if any, of the one-year period from the date of the letter notifying you of the action that you have appealed. If we do not hear from you within this period, we will close your case."

If you received the Statement of the Case within sixty days of the anniversary date of your denial letter, your deadline is the anniversary date. Otherwise, the appeal will automatically be terminated on the expiration date. However, if you are planning to exercise your right to appeal the decision and you need more time to locate and develop further evidence for your appeal, you can write to the VA requesting additional time to submit your Substantive Appeal. More than likely, it will grant the request. The VA does not want to defend an inquiry from your congressional representative about why it denied you due process.

Identify and Discuss All Evidence

The second most important step when you review the Statement of the Case is to make certain the VA addressed *all the evidence you submitted.* Time and time again I have reviewed SOCs in which the VA failed to acknowledge evidence the appellant submitted that strengthen his entitlement to benefits.

The U.S. Court of Appeals for Veterans Claims and the Board of Veterans' Appeals have hammered this legal issue for two decades. Regional Offices must give an adequate statement of reasons or bases when justifying a denial of a claim. The Court has also consistently held that the VA is not free to ignore its own regulations.[4] Similarly, the Court has stated, "Where the rights of individuals are affected, it is incumbent upon agencies to follow their own procedures." Therefore, a VA Decision Review Officer (DRO) at a veteran's personal hearing is required to suggest to the veteran that he submit, or seek to have the VA obtain, medical evidence of the then-current level of his service-connected disability.

In deciding claims for benefits, the BVA is required to provide in its decisions "a written statement of [its] findings and conclusions, and the reasons or bases for those findings and conclusions, on all material issues of fact and law presented on the record."[5] When an asserted basis for an award of VA benefits is "presented on the record," the BVA's or local Regional Office's obligation is to provide a written statement of its findings and conclusions, with reasons or bases therefore. The BVA or Regional Office must explain to the claimant its decision on that claim. The Board (or RO) may not simply ignore a claim for benefits presented on the record before it.

This single issue of providing adequate statement of reasons or bases when justifying the denial of a claim has appeared before the CAVC 3,628 times during the past twenty years. Five hundred and ten of these appeals were

---

4. See *Gilbert v. Derwinski*, 1 Vet.App. 50 (1990).
5. See *Karnas v. Derwinski*, 1 Vet.App. 308, 311 (1991).

decided by a panel of three judges and 3,118 before a single judge. It appears that individuals on both sides of the issue have difficulty applying this concept, which may account for the large number of cases before the U.S. Court of Appeals for Veterans Claims.

Pay Attention to the Medical Evidence of Record

The third step is to compare how the appeals officer treats the medical findings of the VA Medical Center's Compensation and Pension Examination Section and that of your non-VA physicians. If your physicians' findings support your contention for the injury or illness and the C&P Examiner's differs, make certain the Appeals Officer's decision states why your evidence is without merit. Check carefully that the C&P Examiner's findings were based on accepted medical principles and that the examiner's rebuttal was not a personal opinion but rather based on medical principles. This is the scenario that veteran James Rogers discovered when he scrutinized the Statement of the Case.

Medical Principles as Speculations

In the example of James Rogers, the Rating Officer held that the C&P Exam administered by a nurse practitioner was sufficient to deny service connection because she concluded in her summary, "It would be pure speculation that the veteran's heart disease was related to his service." The nurse practitioner further stated, "There were no medical studies or theses to support the veteran's claim." This was her opinion, not a finding based on medical facts. It was also obvious that neither she nor her supervisor had read the veteran's claim file. The findings by a board-certified cardiologist and internist were ignored by the

C&P staff. The Rating Officer justified his decision to deny benefits quoting portions of both physicians' statements out of context.

Countering Bias or Prejudicial Conclusions

Rogers requested that his cardiologist review the Statement of the Case and provide another letter, rebutting the VA nurse practitioner's conclusions as well as those of the Rating Officer, using key words that the VA looks for. The veteran also had another cardiologist review his medical history and the Statement of the Case. These two new statements were noted and attached to his formal appeal. Rogers should have been furnished a Supplement Statement of the Case (per 38 CFR §19.29) when these new medical statements were identified and forwarded as part of the formal appeal. Since the Substantive Appeal had not been certified to the Board of Veterans' Appeals, the Rating Officer's duty was quite clear: he was to issue a Supplement Statement of the Case.

It is possible that the Appeals Officer's action was deliberate. It is also possible that the officer was not able to analyze and comprehend the significance of the veteran's Substantive Appeal. There is another possible explanation: he or she may never have reviewed the Substantive Appeal before signing off on it and shipping it out of the Regional Office for off-site storage.

Cover Letter

In this particular example, the VA furnished veteran Rogers with a Statement of the Case five months subsequent to the filing of the Notice of Disagreement. In this instance the veteran had a four-month and one-week window to file his appeal.

The VA referenced the following paragraphs from 38 CFR Part 3: §3.159 (Sep 03) Department of Veterans Affairs assistance in developing claims; §3.2600 Review of benefit claims decision; §3.303 Principles relating to service connection; §3.307 (Jun 03) Presumptive conditions for wartime and service on or after January 1, 1947; §3.309 (Nov 02) Diseases subject to presumptive service connection; §3.310 Proximate results, secondary conditions. This information will vary on a case by case basis.[6]

The letter sent to James Rogers stated, in part:

> We have enclosed a Statement of the Case, a summary of the law and evidence concerning your claim. This summary will help you to make the best argument to the BVA on why you think our decision should be changed.
>
> What You Need to Do
>
> To complete your appeal, you must file a formal appeal. We have enclosed VA Form 9, Appeal to the Board of Veterans' Appeals, which you may use to complete your appeal. We will gladly explain the form if you have questions. Your appeal should address:
>
> - the benefit you want
> - the facts in the Statement of the Case with which you disagree; and

---

6. The pages 7 through 14 were excluded from this example. These pages were not duplicated because they were a replication of the pertinent paragraphs from 38 CFR Part 3 that were applicable to each individual case.

- the errors that you believe we made in applying the law.

When You Need to Do It

You must file your appeal with this office within sixty days from the date of this letter or within the remainder, if any, of the one-year period from the date of the letter notifying you of the action that you have appealed. If we do not hear from you within this period, we will close your case. If you need more time to file your appeal, you should request more time before the time limit for filing your appeal expires. See item 5 of the instructions in VA Form 9, Appeal to Board of Veterans' Appeals.

Hearings

You may have a hearing before we send your case to the BVA. If you tell us that you want a hearing, we will arrange a time and a place for the hearing. VA will provide the hearing room, the hearing official, and a transcript of the hearing for the record. VA cannot pay any other expenses of the hearing. You may also have a record hearing before the BVA, as noted on the enclosed VA Form 9 Appeal to the Board of Veterans' Appeals. Do not delay filing your appeal if you request a hearing. Your request for a hearing does not extend the time to file your appeal.

Representation

If you do not have a representative, it is not too late to choose one. An accredited representative of a recognized service organization may represent you without charge. An attorney or an accredited agent may also represent you and may charge you a fee for services related to your claim that he or she provides after a final decision of the BVA under certain circumstances. VA cannot pay fees of agents or attorneys. For more information on fees, see 38 USC § 5904. If an attorney or accredited agent charges a fee for services in connection with your claim before VA, the attorney or agent should file a copy of the fee agreement within thirty days after it is signed. The fee agreement should be filed at the following address: Counsel to the Chairman (01C3), Board of Veterans' Appeals, 810 Vermont Avenue, NW, Washington, DC 20420.

What We Will Do

After we receive your appeal, we will send your case to the BVA in Washington, D.C., for a decision. The BVA will base its decision on an independent review of the entire record, including the transcript of the hearing, if you have a hearing.

Justification for Claim Denial

As a rule, the actual justification for denying your claim will usually be the last three or four pages of the SOC. It is a good idea to read this portion of the Statement of the Case several times. Make notes as you read the VA's rationale for denying service connection for the disabilities claimed.

In Rogers's case here is part of the VA's rationale, which he disagreed with and would counter in his formal appeal:

- Implied that shortness of breath was an occasional medical event that would occur only if I participated in extreme exercising. Their rationale was completely silent as to what constituted extreme exercising.

- The Rating Team concluded the EKG in June 1990 was within normal limits therefore there was no heart disease. However, the rater ignored other evidence such as night leg pains, chest pain, and shortness of breath coupled with chronic gum disease, exposure to high-decibel sound for several decades, and irregular work hours, including shift work, as factors that silently cause heart disease. One of the first subtle signs of heart disease is the repolization of the T wave when it is inverted.

- The rater failed to address or rebut twenty-seven medical theses and studies that I submitted showing that my coronary artery disease, more likely than not, started while I was on active duty. The rater totally ignored a paper published by the Mayo Clinic that stated, "coronary-artery disease develops slowly and silently over decades. It can go virtually unnoticed until it produces a heart attack."

- Three statements were furnished from three board-certified physicians stating that my active-duty medical history indicated that I had the early stages of coronary artery disease while on active duty. The one physician who was ignored stated, "The patient had atherosclerotic heart disease in 1990."

- The rater accepted a nurse practitioner's statement that tipped the scale of preponderance of evidence against me when she opined that there was no literature, studies, or theses that would support my claim. She held that to grant service connection would be based on pure speculation.

- The Rating Officer misinformed me that service connection was denied because it was not diagnosed within one year of my leaving the service. What the law states is that the condition must *manifest* itself within one year after leaving the service to a degree of 10 percent. I did in fact demonstrate and document these symptoms two years before I retired from the service. The law says nothing about my needing a formal diagnosis within one year after leaving the service to be granted service connection.

- The Rating Officer accepted a C&P Examiner's opinion without any medical evidence to support her conclusions contrary to the intent of VA regulation 38 CFR §4.2 Interpretation of Examination Reports.

James Rogers would not have been able to prepare a formal appeal if he had not obtained copies of all records and researched pertinent regulations and medical facts pertaining to his claim.

Analyze the Rating Decision

After you have filed a Notice of Disagreement and received a Statement of the Case, your next big step is studying the rating decision. A rating decision is a statement issued by the VA that explains why a Ratings Team member denied or granted compensation benefits. *Read the decision completely and understand every term that is used.* If a Regional Office has ten Ratings Officers assigned to rate claims, these claims will be reviewed and interpreted in ten different ways. Rating a claim is a slanted process because it reflects the rater's personal competence, education, and experience when deciding legal and medical issues.

Organize the Evidence You Collected

After reading the rating decision, your mission is to assemble a well-organized appeal based on hard evidence, sworn statements, medical theses, VA medical and C&P Examinations, and military health and hospital records. Since the VA does not store your records in chronological order, you will have to organize your files when you have received them. Sort this material in your records by subject and date. Once the information is grouped by subject, organize it by date. This exercise will focus the appeals team, or the BVA's administrative judge, on the evidence that establishes your entitlement.

Outline the Evidentiary Facts

It is best to start with an outline of what your objectives are for each issue you are claiming is service-connected. Keep in mind when organizing your evidence that you need to prove *three* conditions: in-service occurrence, the condition currently exists, and a link between your active-duty medical problems and your current conditions exists.

In veteran Rogers's case, his symptoms were first

recorded two years before he retired from the service. His initial outline might look like this:

Issue 1: Cardiovascular disease

- In-service occurrence
- In-service medical records reflecting the disease had manifested to a degree of 10 percent or more prior to retirement or separation.

Arrange your records from the earliest date to the date of separation.

- Post-service treatment of the disease
- Hospital records of triple bypass surgery resulting from heart attack to include emergency room records, operation records, and doctor summaries
- Current treatment records from cardiologist
- Letter from cardiologist stating that current heart problems are more likely than not related to military service
- Common link between in-service and post-service diagnosis to establish service connection
- Hospital records for the seventeen times I was hospitalized for my heart
- Reasons why four stents were inserted into arteries
- Medical theses establishing how my heart problems are service-related
- Statements from family and spouse reflecting the changes and physical limitations they observed
- Regulations and statutes pertinent to establishing service connection

Issue 2: Depression and anxiety secondary to heart attack

- In-service occurrence
- Not applicable because depression and anxiety were the results of the heart attack
- Post-service treatment of the disease
- Provide copies of mental health examinations that establish that I experienced mental health issues because of my heart attack
- Medical theses establishing that a serious health trauma could trigger chronic depression and anxiety
- Copies of medication prescribed to treat depression and anxiety
- Common link in post-service diagnosis to establish service connection
- VA regulation that mandates establishing service connection when the primary in-service condition causes a secondary disability
- Decisions by the Court of Appeals for Veterans Claims and the Board of Veterans' Appeals that mandates when benefits should be granted for secondary health problems caused by a primary condition that occurred on active duty

Issue 3: Service connection for tinnitus

- In-service occurrence
- Proof I spent twenty-three years in and around aircraft
- Post-service treatment of the disease
- Loud ringing in my ears
- C&P Audio Examiner determined from test and proof of military assignment that more likely

than not tinnitus is service-related

- Common link in post-service diagnosis to establish service connection
- Will prove that since my retirement from the service I have not been subjected to any high-decibel sounds that could cause tinnitus

Issue 4: Service connection for bilateral hearing loss

- In-service occurrence
- Proof veteran Rogers spent twenty-three years in and around aircraft
- Post-service treatment of the disease
- Audio test shows sharp loss of hearing at the mid- to high-decibel range. C&P Audio Examiner determined from test and proof of military assignments that it is more likely than not the hearing loss is service-related.

Keep in mind that this general outline should be expanded to identify the evidence that is relevant in each subgroup and should also be arranged by date.

Completing the Substantive Appeal

Your appeal brief is an organized written statement explaining why you should be granted service-connected benefits for your injury or illness. It is now time to use that valuable information concerning your service-related injuries or diseases and explain why you disagree with the VA's decision. When preparing your appeal, keep these objectives in mind:

- The appeal must focus the Decision Review Officer's or the Board of Veterans' Appeals judge's attention on the facts that prove entitlement for you and point to the faulty conclusions and actions by the Ratings Officer to execute his or her duties in accordance with the statutes, regulations, case law, and policy of the Department of Veterans Affairs.

- If you obtained additional evidence that pertains to your claim, it must be attached to your appeal and accepted by the Appeals Officer. You will note how to introduce this evidence from James R. Rogers's appeal.

- From your copy of the rating decision, use the names of each individual who was responsible for your claim being denied. In the example of the Substantive Appeal provided, note how the veteran identified the incorrect action by Ratings Officer Ms. Irene Dunn, Appeals Officer James Lincoln, and DRO Ira Wright. Since you have to show proof of these allegations, guard against expressing a personal opinion rather than making a statement of fact.

Next you want to present your table of authorities, a table of contents for a legal document used to argue your appeal. It is a list of legal references to other court cases, statutes, rules, citations, regulations, and amendments that supports your arguments referenced in your Substantive Appeal. When preparing a table of authorities, note the page number of the reference in your appeal. This is explained further in Part III of this book.

The next section in this book will explain what errors

you, the veteran, may need to address and correct. Following is a section on potential VA errors and what you need to do to submit a successful claims appeal.

PART 1

THE VETERAN'S ERRORS—BEFORE AND AFTER FILING

FAILURE TO UNDERSTAND THE CLAIMING PROCESS

The most important point to keep in mind when filing a claim is that obtaining benefits for a service-connected disability is tedious and time-consuming. It is not a simple process of answering questions on a form, submitting that form to the Department of Veterans Affairs, and receiving service-connection benefits a few months later.

The VA is required by the Duty to Assist Act to help you obtain evidence before it rates your claim; however, assistance is limited because of the volume of claims submitted to the VA. The VA is supposed to acquire a copy of your DD-214 to establish that you were in the service, your outpatient medical records, and various other military records, but you alone are responsible for making sure the VA actually collects those documents and for providing enough evidence to make your case.

The information collected by the VA will not be enough to substantiate your claim. You must tell the VA what kind of additional evidence there is and where it might be found. This is a daunting and perplexing task for many veterans. Thus, it is understandable that many claims are denied, leading many determined, and often confused, veterans to begin the appeals process. In order to make a successful appeal, you must understand both the claims and appeals processes. For a detailed explanation of the appeals process, read the section of this book titled "The Appeals Process: Step by Step."

FAILURE TO KNOW WHEN ADVICE FROM THE VA IS NOT GOOD

If you are told to simply fill out the appeal or claim form and leave the rest to the VA, this is not good advice. If you leave it up to the VA to decide your case based on the information it collects, you make it easier for the VA to deny your claim or appeal.

Do not take the instructions on item 10 on VA Form 9 Appeal to the Board of Veterans' Appeals literally when it asks you to respond to the prompt, "Here is why I think the VA decided my case incorrectly." You cannot merely say, "I was injured while serving overseas in Iraq and there is proof in my military records." In small print the form says, "Continue on the back, or attach sheets of paper, if you need more space." You should attach a well-organized and documented portfolio of substantiating evidence if you want to present a successful appeal; a half or even full sheet of paper will not be enough. You have to prove that the Rating Team member incorrectly interpreted the medical facts and supporting evidence of your case and that the laws and regulations pertaining to your claim clearly support your arguments. Do not be vague in your formal appeal. Even if the BVA judge sympathizes with you and wants to grant you service connection, he cannot vacate the Regional Office's decision without a well-documented argument that the proves the Rating Officer failed to interpret the evidence correctly.

PROBABILITY OF WINNING YOUR APPEAL

Given these three scenarios in regard to the VA Form 9, what are the odds that you will win your appeal with the VA?

To complete the form, you ask your service officer from your local DAV, VFW, or American Legion, or a County Veteran Service Officer to fill out your claim form and submit it to the VA.
Probability of a successful appeal: **LOW**

In the spaces provided, you complete all the requested information on the VA Form 9, including the answer to why you believe the VA decided your case incorrectly.You submit the form to the VA.
Probability of a successful appeal: **LOW**

Accompanying the VA Form 9 is your well-organized portfolio of complete documentation relating to your claim. This includes supporting medical evidence and a treatment timeline, and fully substantiates your injury or illness claim.
Probablity of a successful appeal: **HIGH**

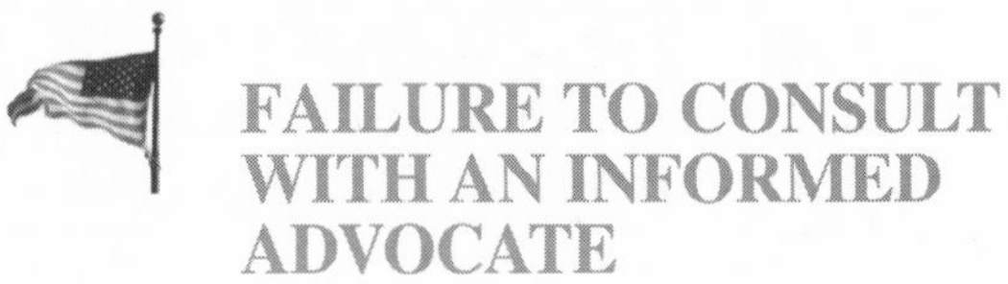

FAILURE TO CONSULT WITH AN INFORMED ADVOCATE

If you decide to employ an advocate to assist you in submitting your appeal, make sure you hire someone who is experienced and trained to work with the VA. There is too much at risk for you to select a Service Officer to handle your case at random.

Training Is Limited

Service Officers from the local DAV, VFW, American Legion, or County Veteran Service Office receive training each year based on VA guidelines, but that does not mean they know what evidence is necessary to make a successful appeal. They are not taught how to find evidence, research court decisions, or locate medical theses pertinent to your injury or illness. Furthermore, they do not have access to all the significant VA regulations or manuals. Despite their good intentions, most Service Officers representing the VA in your community can offer only minimal assistance because their training is limited.

Gifted Advocates Are Out There

In all fairness, there are some fantastically dedicated and knowledgeable Service Officers. For the veterans they represent, they go the whole nine yards and have a history of successful claims and appeals actions. Make sure the person you select to help you is a well-trained and knowledgeable individual who will develop and argue your claim or appeal successfully. You do not want to hire an advocate who can only fill out VA forms.

Attorneys

In 2007 Congress passed the Veterans' Benefit Protection Act, which allows veterans to seek representation by an attorney once the VA has denied benefits. Many veterans service organizations object to this act because veterans' benefits may be slowed or diminished in value after lawyer fees. Several service organizations have pressed Congress to repeal this act. There are numbers of resources, free of cost, available to veterans who need assistance with claims, including local veterans organizations and congressional offices. To locate an attorney who is experienced in veterans and military law, either log on to the U.S. Court of Appeals for Veterans Claims website and search for attorneys who practice before this court or contact the local bar association for a possible referral.

WHAT TO LOOK FOR IN AN ADVOCATE

- Look for an advocate who has successfully represented others before the Board of Veterans' Appeals. Ask the advocate how many appeals he or she has filed and how many cases he or she has won.
- Ask how long the advocate has represented veterans before a Decision Review Officer review or the BVA.
- Ask about the advocate's ability to access

continued on next page

continued from previous page

VA manuals, regulations, U.S. Codes, and case law.

- Determine the advocate's understanding of the complexities associated with the medical and legal issues pertaining to your case.

- Ask how he or she will present your case before a DRO or a BVA judge.

- Ask about the advocate's ability to prepare an appeal. Request to see an example of the type of brief the advocate would file on your behalf.

- Make certain your advocate can state arguments clearly and write concisely.

- Inquire about the advocate's capability to research using the Internet.

- Determine whether the advocate knows medical experts who will evaluate you and review your active-duty medical history.

- If so, determine if the physician will point out any medical inaccuracies that could prejudice the medical conclusions of the C&P Examination.

- Determine if the advocate will represent you before the BVA.
- Determine if he will hold a prehearing DRO or BVA meeting to ascertain that all the key issues are covered.

FAILURE TO SUBSTANTIATE THE CLAIM

Properly supporting an appeal requires facts that cannot be rebutted or dismissed as speculation by a Rating Team member. You are appealing because you failed to substantiate your original claim with corroborating evidence. The term *substantive* means "[to] establish the existence or truth of, by true or competent evidence or to verify." Nothing is easier for the VA to rate, and ultimately deny, than an unsubstantiated claim. A successful claim or appeal provides substantiated evidence that satisfies the four basic elements of a claim.

- **Proof of Service**—Prove you were in the military.
- **Proof of Service Occurrenc**e—Provide evidence that the injury or illness you are claiming occurred while you were on active duty. This is

also known as establishing a nexus. *Note:* the VA must accept your explanation that your injury is service-related if your service records show you have a Combat Infantry Badge, Purple Heart, Bronze Star, and Air Medal with V Device, along with other awards and decorations. This cuts out all the guesswork on the VA's part, as it has to evaluate only the degree of disability based on the medical evidence.

- **Continuity of Symptomatology**—If your claim is not filed within one year of leaving the service or the medical condition is not universally accepted as being a medically chronic condition, you must prove that you have been continuously treated for the injury or illness for which you are seeking benefits. Here are some ways to locate a former doctor:

  Reed Reference Publishing Company
  Directory of Board-Certified Medical Specialists
  AMA Website
  Department of Professional Licensing
  State AMA Chapter
  Internet White and Yellow Pages

- **Proof of Current Disability—**Show that you are currently disabled as a result of the service-related medical condition for which you are seeking benefits.

If you cannot substantiate the injury or illness to satisfy each of these elements, your claim or appeal will be denied. Substantive evidence includes records, such as military medical and unit history records, documents such as a line of duty (LOD) investigation or an after-action report, and sworn statements from other service members who have firsthand knowledge of the incident. Become a Paper PI; track down as much evidence as possible. The more substantial evidence you present, the more likely it is that your appeal will be successful.

FAILURE TO PROVIDE SECONDARY EVIDENCE

When primary evidence cannot be located, you must focus on building your appeal on secondary evidence. For example, copies of unit historical records often provide details of unit casualties that can substantiate a combat-related injury; unit morning reports or PDCs will provide duty status for any given day; if you were hospitalized, the records will show the period of hospitalization but not why you were hospitalized; an official LOD investigation is an excellent source for substantiating an injury.

If you were, or think you might have been, exposed to biological agents, radiation, or various types of mind-controlling drugs, you can request records from government agencies under the provisions of the Freedom of Information Act. Thousands of individuals have likely not realized they were exposed to such chemicals. If you have been exposed and can prove it, you could be entitled to compensation benefits for the health problems created by exposure to these chemicals.

Secondary Evidence

The following is a list of records that could provide secondary evidence to aid in substantiating your claim:

Military Historical Archives—Historical records kept on each branch of the service by the Department of Defense
Special Military Searches
Morning Reports
Unit Historical Records
Organizational History Files, 1980 to Present
U.S. Army Institute of Heraldry—Contains unofficial material such as unit histories, personal papers, diaries, and photographs including certain select official papers.
Outpatient Medical Records
Defense Special Weapons Agency (DSWA)
Unofficial Unit Records
Occupational Radiation Exposure Documents
Office of Human Radiation Experiments (OHRE)

Sworn Statements

Sworn statements from you, family, friends, employers, and former military buddies are hard evidence that the VA must consider and weigh during the adjudication process. The VA must accept and treat sworn statements as it would any other form of evidence related to the claim; the VA cannot question the validity of sworn statements. When properly executed, a statement from a third party (lay evidence) can be important in the adjudication process. It is just as important as service medical records, post-service doctor's assessments, or any other form of evidence when building a well-grounded appeal. Providing any or all of the following types of sworn statements will help strengthen your appeal.

Sworn Statement by Spouse
Sworn Statement by Employer

Sworn Statement by Former Comrades
Sworn Statement by Veteran

Witnesses

To search for witnesses, the following are helpful resources in locating former comrades or military personnel who would strengthen your appeal:

Department of Veterans Affairs
Department of State
Newspaper classifieds
Magazines for veterans and active-duty personnel
Auto Licensing
Books on how to look for a lost friend or family member
National Archives and Records Administration (NARA)—The NARA archives documents and records for all government agencies. Thus, it is one of the most valuable sources of primary and secondary evidence to support a claim or an appeal.

FAILURE TO RESEARCH MEDICAL ISSUES

If you cannot rebut the conclusions of a VA C&P Evaluation with solid published medical evidence, you will most likely lose your appeal. The advent of the Internet has made it easy to research your medical problem so that you understand the complexities of your injury or illness and how it does, or could, affect your life. The detailed information you assemble from known sources qualifies as sound secondary evidence that will strengthen your appeal and protect you from random opinions within the medical community, which could be used against you.

The U.S. Court of Appeals for Veterans Claims has held that the VA must consider all evidence submitted by the appellant. Therefore, your evidence cannot be dismissed solely because it is obtained from the Internet; however, your research must come from a recognized authority. Start your search with sources such as the Center for Disease Control, the National Institutes of Health (NIH), military medical manuals, medical textbooks, and medical journals. You can even attach a copy of a medical study conducted in England that is accepted by the medical profession at large. If the VA rebuts the finding of any study, it has to come up with hard medical

FREQUENTLY ASKED QUESTIONS (FAQ)

Military Personnel Records

Access to Records by Veterans, Next-of-Kin, or the Veteran's Representative

Copies of most military and medical records on file at NPRC-MPR, including the DD Form 214, Report of Separation (or equivalent), can be made available upon request. Veterans and next-of-kin of deceased veterans have the same rights to full access to the record. Next-of-kin are the unremarried widow or widower, son or daughter, father or mother, brother or sister of the deceased veteran.

evidence to prove the study is unfounded.

In addition to requiring the BVA to consider all evidence on record, the U.S. Court of Appeals for Veterans Claims ruled the BVA must also consider, and discuss in its decision, all potentially applicable provisions of law and regulation. The Board must analyze the credibility and probative value of the evidence, account for the evidence that it finds persuasive or unpersuasive, and provide a written statement explaining its reasoning or bases for its findings and conclusions for its rejection of any material evidence favorable to the claimant. The written statement must adequately enable an appellant to understand the precise bases for the Board's decision as well as facilitate informed review by the Court.

Authorized third-party requesters, e.g., lawyers, doctors, historians, etc., may submit requests for information from individual records with the veteran's (or next of kin's) signed and dated authorization. All authorizations should specify exactly what the veteran (or next-of-kin) is allowing to be released to a third party. Authorizations are valid one year from the date of signature.

Information or copies of documents may be released from Official Military Personnel Files within the provisions of the law. The Freedom of Information Act and the Privacy Act provide balance between the right of the public to obtain information from military service records, and the right of the former military service member to protect his or her privacy. Please

continued on next page

continued from previous page

review these items for additional information. In all cases, you must sufficiently identify the person whose record is requested, so that the records can be located with reasonable effort.

Preparing Requests for Information from Official Military Personnel Files

Federal law [5 USC 552a(b)] requires that all requests for records and information be submitted in writing. Each request must be *signed* (in cursive) and *dated* (within the last year).

Requests must contain enough information to identify the record among the more than 70 million on file at NPRC-MPR. Certain basic information is needed to locate military service records. This information includes the veteran's complete name used while in service, service number, social security number, branch of service, and dates of service. Date and place of birth may also be helpful, especially if the service number is not known. If the request pertains to a record that may have been involved in the 1973 fire, also include place of discharge, last unit of assignment, and place of entry into the service, if known.

Veterans who plan to file a claim for medical benefits with the Department of Veterans Affairs do not need to request a copy of their military health record from NPRC-MPR. The original health records are provided by the center when requested by the VA after the claim is filed. Many health records were lent to the Department of Veterans Affairs prior to the 1973 fire.

Veterans who filed a medical claim should contact the Department of Veterans Affairs in order to determine if their record is already on file. The VA toll free number is 1-800-827-1000. This number will connect the caller to the nearest VA office.

To request military service records, veterans and the next-of-kin of ***deceased*** veterans may use vetrecs .archives.gov. For all others, the Standard Form (SF) 180, Request Pertaining to Military Records, although not mandatory, is the recommended method to send a request for military service information. This form captures all the necessary information to locate a record. Provide as much information on the form as possible and send copies of any service documents that you may have. Requests may also be submitted as a letter containing the basic information listed above.

Follow the instructions for preparing the SF 180. Check the table to determine the location of the record and submit your request to the appropriate address.

Note: Do not use the addresses on the SF 180 for sending requests related to the issuance or replacement of medals and awards. Military Awards and Decorations provides the correct mailing addresses for submitting correspondence for issuance or replacement.

Costs

Generally, there is no charge for military personnel and health record information provided to veterans,

continued on next page

continued from previous page

next-of-kin, and authorized representatives. If your request involves a service fee, you will be notified as soon as that determination is made.

Response Time

Response time varies dependent on the complexity of your request, the availability of records, and the NPRC-MPR's workload. Please do not send a follow-up request before ninety days have elapsed as it may cause further delays. ●

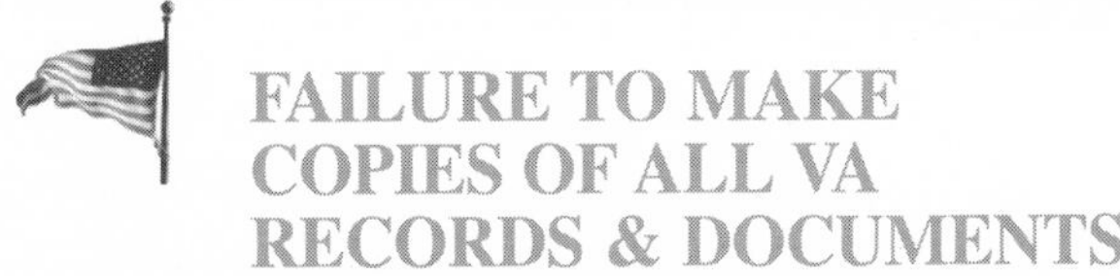

FAILURE TO MAKE COPIES OF ALL VA RECORDS & DOCUMENTS

If you failed to acquire copies of all VA records and documents during the claim process, you must obtain a copy of every piece of paper pertaining to your time at the VA and in the military when gathering evidence to make your appeal. The only way to convince the VA that you are entitled to benefits is by supporting your claim with solid evidence, which includes all medical documents and records. The process may seem overwhelming at first, but if you take it one step at a time it will be manageable.

To plan a winning strategy, you must know what the VA knows and what additional evidence will be necessary to support your appeal. First, request a copy of your claim file under the provisions of the FOIA. Ask for copies of all documents, medical records, rating decisions, C&P Examination results, AMIE instructions to the C&P examining facility, VA Form 626 Remarks by Accredited Representative, and military health records that comprise your file. The most acceptable way to request copies of records from the VA is to state your request on VA Form 21-4138. This form may be used when requesting copies of information from your claim file and when requesting copies of treatment records from a VA Medical Center or Clinic. To increase the likelihood of obtaining your medical records, provide the representative at the storage site with the name of the hospital where you were treated and when you were a patient.

When you have obtained all of your missing records, immediately request official copies. You may also ask your congressional representative to send for copies of those records on your behalf. To find records for a previously denied claim, a claim you want to amend, or to request an increase to an existing disability rating, contact the RO who was custodian of the claim file.

FAILURE TO ACQUIRE COPIES OF MILITARY SERVICE & HEALTH RECORDS

Failure to obtain copies of your military documents and health records will be detrimental to your case. Retiree active-duty health records are sent to the Military Personnel Records Division of the National Personnel Records Center from facilities of all military services after one to three years of inactivity and are retained by the NPRC-MPR for fifty years from the last patient activity. The medical facility's records administrator will advise you of whether your records are still under its control or whether they were transferred to the NPRC-MPR and, if so, when. If the date of last treatment at a military facility was less than three years ago, the retiree's first inquiry for copies of health records should be to the facility that provided the treatment.

Military health records maintained by the NPRC-MPR are divided into two categories: Official Military Personnel Files (OMPF) and inpatient hospital records. OMPF, including outpatient hospital records, can be requested from the NPRC-MPR using their form SF-180. Inpatient hospital records are stored separately from OMPF and outpatient health records. To obtain a copy of inpatient records you must submit a special request to the NPRC-MPR, preferably using NA Form 13042 Request for Information Needed to Locate Medical Records. If you are unable to obtain this form, the following information is essential for the NPRC-MPR to help provide a copy of your hospital records: name, serial number, social security number, military hospital where treated, period of hospitalization, and medical problem for which you were hospitalized. When identifying the military hospital, identify the branch of service that administers the hospital care.

FAILURE TO KEEP A SUSPENSE DATE

If you fail to respond within the given suspense period to the VA's request for more information, the claim decision will be final on the one-year anniversary date the VA issued the denial of benefits letter. The only exception is if you can show that you were physically or mentally incapacitated during that time period. Letters from the VA can be confusing; therefore, it is important to read letters from the VA with great care and to note important dates. Failure to respond within the given suspense period not only jeopardizes your claim but also gives you less time to file a formal appeal.

The One-Year Suspense Date

There are two times you will receive a one-year suspense date. You will first receive a one-year suspense date, which begins on the date of separation, to file a claim for any injury or illness. If the claim is granted, the date is retroactively adjusted to the date you left the service. The law states that any condition that results in observable symptoms within one year following separation from the service will be considered service-related. Remember, to be granted benefits the symptoms merely have to be observable, not diagnosed. If you receive a letter from the VA denying benefits because the injury or disease was not diagnosed within one year of your discharge from military service, submit a Notice of Disagreement.

A one-year suspense date will also be issued as the time frame you have to file a NOD if your claim was denied and you want to appeal the ruling. Once that year expires, the VA's decision becomes final, which makes reopening your case challenging.

The Sixty-Day Suspense Date

Many veterans are not aware there are also several sixty-day suspense dates to which they must pay attention. If you have a claim pending and the VA requests that you provide it with some sort of evidence, form, or statement,

THE GAO REPORT TO CONGRESS 2002

The U.S. Government Accountability Office (GAO) presented a report to Congress in April 2002 that stated,

> [T]he clarity of letters to claimants needs to be improved. . . . [K]ey aspects that claimants needed to understand were unclear. About half of [the Veterans Benefits Administration's] compensation letters did not clearly explain pertinent financial information concerning the claimants' benefit. Similarly, nearly 30 percent of compensation letters did not clearly explain the reason for VBA's decision regarding whether or not to award benefits. Among the letters that did not clearly explain the reason for the decision, many had legal and medical terminology in the attached rating decision document that would be difficult for a layperson to understand. Further, about 43 percent of the development letters did not clearly explain the actions that claimants were to take to support their claims. Beyond the lack of clarity in these key aspects of the letters, various writing deficiencies, such as sequencing and formatting problems, reduced the overall clarity of VBA's letters.

and you fail to respond within thirty days or sixty days, depending on the purpose of the letter, you will more than likely receive a letter explaining that your claim has been rated based on the evidence in your file. The letter states that the decision is final if you fail to respond before the one-year anniversary date of your *original claim*, not one year from the date the decision letter was issued. Therefore, it is of the utmost importance that you read letters from the VA carefully and note important dates.

FAILURE TO ENSURE YOUR INFORMATION WAS RECEIVED ON TIME

To determine the crucial date of a response, the VA credits the date of receipt when it is date-stamped into the Regional Office. There are several steps you can take to ensure your response does not get lost in the system. If you send it by mail, make certain you send it by certified mail and request a return receipt (Postal forms 3800 and 3811). This gives you proof that the evidence or information was sent before the suspense date expired.

Another way of protecting yourself, especially if you are close to a deadline, is to take your evidence and information to your congressional representative's office and ask him or her to fax it to the Regional Office. Request that he or she follows up the fax by mailing the hard copy of the material to the Regional Office. Once an action gets into congressional channels, the VA pays special attention to the requests and has to accept the date and time of the fax as your response date.

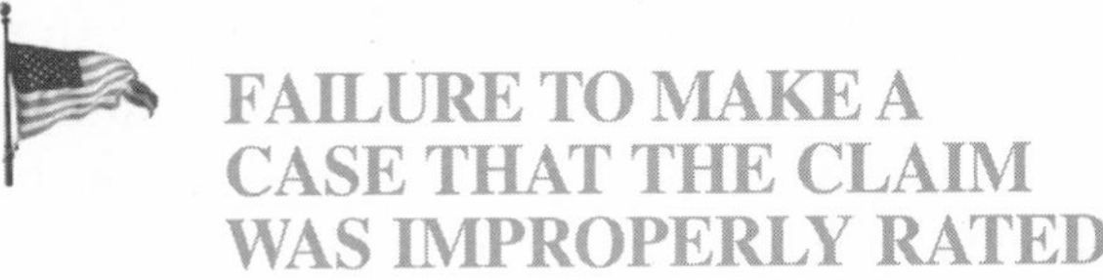

FAILURE TO MAKE A CASE THAT THE CLAIM WAS IMPROPERLY RATED

Veterans often feel that claim ratings are lower than what they are physically experiencing; therefore, when you receive your rating, ask yourself if your claim was properly rated. In the 2005 fiscal year, 63 percent of all rated claims received a disability rating of 30 percent or less. Forty-four percent of these were rated only 10 percent disabling.

If you believe you were awarded a lower disability rating than you deserve, obtain a complete evaluation from a non-VA medical source. Give your medical specialist a copy of the VA's C&P Examination, the VA rating decision, a copy of the appropriate Disability Examination Worksheet, and a copy of the pertinent subchapters in 38 CFR Part 4. Ask that a statement be prepared by the medical specialist in which he or she testifies to the disability rating he or she would assign you based on VA guidelines and the reasoning behind his or her conclusion. Though the examination costs a few hundred dollars, you could gain a lifetime of increased compensation benefits.

FAILURE TO ASK FOR A HEARING BEFORE A DRO OR BVA JUDGE

If you have already been through the appeals process once and wonder why your appeal was denied, it could have been because you did not ask for a hearing. Your chances of making a successful appeal are greatly improved if you can state your case before the agency of original jurisdiction, the DRO. You can request such a hearing prior to the filing of a formal appeal. The DRO is a senior adjudicator who has the authority to reverse an RO's decision to deny benefits if you can persuade him or her that the evidence was misinterpreted.

The DRO can only consider the evidence the RO used to deny your claim. All new evidence must be submitted to the RO for evaluation. If the evidence does not enable the RO to grant you benefits, he or she must provide you with a Supplement Statement of the Case (SSOC), which must present a detailed explanation of why this evidence is not relevant. If the RO does not send an SSOC within a reasonable period of time, enlist the aid of your congressional representative.

BVA Hearing Options

When initiating a formal appeal (VA Form 9), you are given three choices to state your intentions: "(a) I do not want a BVA hearing; (b) I want a hearing in Washington, D.C.; (c) I want a BVA hearing at the local VA Office before a member, or members, of the BVA." The option you choose will determine the best implementation strategy.

Forgoing a BVA Hearing

Turning down a BVA hearing is not recommended. If you turn down a hearing, you leave your Substantive Appeal, as filed, as your only advocate. If you have difficultly expressing yourself in writing, you will be severely disadvantaged if you do not request a BVA hearing. The BVA hearing has several benefits. First, it is your only opportunity for personal interaction with the BVA. During the hearing, the judge can ask you specific questions about your appeal, and you can clarify his or her understanding of your arguments in person. Second, your testimony is a sworn statement and can be used as a positive piece of evidence in your denied claim appeal. Finally, during a hearing you may submit additional evidence that was not part of your original filing to further substantiate your claim. You should absolutely not forgo a BVA hearing opportunity.

Hearing in Washington, D.C.

A hearing in Washington, D.C., is the most expensive option. There are multiple travel costs associated with this type of hearing. Unless you live in Virginia or Maryland, which are adjacent to the District, lodging, food, and transportation costs could easily cause a cash crunch. Additionally, if you have a local attorney representing you, his expenses must be added into the total cost. If you elect to be represented by a service organization located in Washington, D.C., you have to consider its ability put together arguments and evaluate your evidence in a short period of time; the Service Officer will have only a few hours at most to digest the facts of your appeal and prepare his or her remarks before the hearing. Also, there will not be enough time for you to participate in planning the strategy to defend your appeal.

Hearing at Local VA Office

There are two ways to conduct a hearing before a BVA judge at the closest Regional Office. The first way is to personally appear before a traveling judge. The second way is to appear before a judge on closed-circuit TV. For this option you go to your local Regional Office and your hearing is performed via videoconference with a BVA judge in the District. Videoconferencing is not available at all Regional Offices, so check with your local office to see if it is a possibility in your area. Choosing either local hearing option will eliminate many of the potential problems and expenses of a hearing in Washington, D.C.

Representation at Your Hearing

Although it is not required, you may engage the services of a veteran's service organization, an agent, or an attorney to represent your interests during your BVA hearing. You want someone who is well-versed in VA law, who is articulate and can accurately depict the facts of the case verbally or in writing, and who has a successful record representing veterans before the board.

PART 2

THE DEPARTMENT OF VETERANS AFFAIRS ERRORS— BEFORE AND AFTER FILING

There are many explanations for why the Department of Veterans Affairs may deny or improperly rate your claim. If in reviewing your records, documents, and medical evaluations, you find that the VA overlooked items in your claim for benefits, you should consider reopening it for the purpose of appealing the denial of benefits or the improperly rated claim. Keep in mind, though, that righting a VA wrong may be out of your control. The department is a bureaucracy, and like any other large organization, it has both strengths and weaknesses. Also, as you read in Part 1, you too may be responsible for your claim being denied. By carefully examining your file and ensuring that all necessary documents and evidence are accounted for, you are taking the right steps toward a successful appeal.

FAILURE TO PROTECT ALL DOCUMENTS & RECORDS

The Regional Office receives thousands of pieces of

mail every day, which must be sorted and forwarded to the correct addressee within each Regional Office. Most claim actions are forwarded to the Triage Team. It determines whether your claim can be processed or if more data is needed. If your claim is complete, the claim application and supporting documents are then physically forwarded to the Predetermination Team.

The Predetermination Team decides when a claim is ready for a final decision by securing the needed evidence. This team is responsible for gathering all military and medical records in government archives as well as any records or reports from nongovernment agencies or knowledgeable individuals who were noted on the application for benefits. If necessary, the Predetermination Team will also schedule a medical examination to assess the nature and severity of your disability.

Next, the Rating Team receives the claim and accompanying documents and reviews the file. Based on your records and the examination, the Rating Team will determine the nature and severity of your injury, whether the injury was incurred during active military duty, and whether it presently affects your day-to-day life. A Rating Officer then prepares a decision citing the evidence and reasons for approval or denial. If the rating is above 0 percent, you will be authorized payments and granted access to the VA's healthcare facilities.

Finally, the Post-determination Team alerts you to the decision and then prepares an award of benefits if you have been approved or sends you a disallowance document if you have been denied.

If the VA is missing documents, it is mostly likely because the Predetermination Team misfiled them. Misfiling is particularly common when additional supporting evidence or statements are sent in. Also, a claim file may have been misrouted if it was physically sent from the Regional Office to the VA Medical Center to be reviewed by a C&P Examiner before a scheduled examination. A document or a new piece of evidence may become separated from the file if it was not properly secured in the folder. Once the C&P Examination is completed and published, the file is once again physically transferred back to the Regional Office.

To ensure that your materials are not lost or misfiled while circulating in the VA, have your congressional representative forward all correspondence, forms, or documents to the Regional Office for you. Remember, the VA has special handling procedures when processing a request from Congress. And *always* make copies of everything you send to the VA.

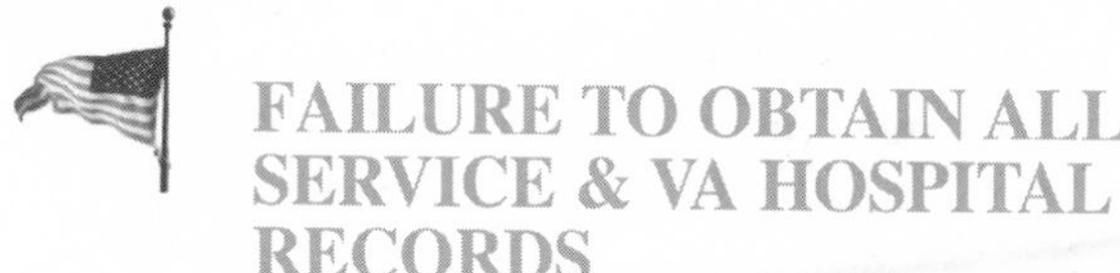

FAILURE TO OBTAIN ALL SERVICE & VA HOSPITAL RECORDS

The VA has a lawful duty to obtain your medical records before initially rating your claim. For example, if you informed the VA that you received treatment for an injury or an illness, the law mandates that the VA obtain those medical records. This action is known as the Duty to Assist. As a matter of law, the VA cannot rate the claim until this duty has been fulfilled. If the VA did not secure your medical records, the BVA judge will remand the original decision back to the Regional Office with instructions to obtain the records. However, you and the VA are responsible for making certain that all in-service and military hospital treatment records are in the claim file before proceeding with your appeal.

FAILURE TO FOLLOW UP ON REQUESTS FOR DOCUMENTS

The VA's Duty to Assist includes securing all the evidence you noted before your claim was forwarded to the RO for a decision. The VA may have failed to follow up on requests for records from other federal agencies. If those agencies do not respond by the deadline given, the Predetermination Team may assume no records exist to substantiate your claim and will forward your claim to the Rating Team without waiting for that evidence. You may be sent a letter stating that an agency has not responded to a request for information. You then may be advised that you have sixty days to obtain this information from that agency (or another source) or your claim will be forwarded to the Rating Team without the additional evidence.

Tenacity in your resolve to find evidence that substantiates how the injury or traumatic event was incurred in the service is integral to appealing the original decision. Request a copy of all your records from the VA or National Personnel Records Center. As previously mentioned, you are entitled to these records under the provision of the FOIA. It states, "this act allows for the full or partial disclosure of previously unreleased information and documents controlled by the U.S. government." If you plan to build a case for the appeal of your denied claim, you will succeed only if you have the records and evidence the VA used to deny your original claim.

FREQUENTLY REQUESTED RECORDS

That Are NOT at the National Personnel Records Center–Military Personnel Records

Department of Veterans Affairs (VA) records. For further information call the VA toll free number: 1-800-827-1000.

Pay records. If available at all, these would be at the various Department of Defense Finance Centers.

Records of veterans who have been separated from active service, but have reserve status, either active or inactive. Contact the reserve component of the appropriate branch of service.

Records of veterans who have been discharged, retired, or who died in service since 1995 (Navy), 1999 (Marine Corps), or 2005 (Air Force). Contact the Personnel Center or Headquarters of the appropriate branch of service. The army has also not retired records of veterans who have been discharged, retired, or who died in service since October 1, 2002, but the National Personnel Records Center has access to those records and will service your requests.

Records of members currently in the National Guard. Contact the Adjutant General's office of the appropriate state. The National Guard Bureau website contains additional information.

continued on next page

continued from previous page

Records of former National Guard members who were not called into active federal service. Contact the Adjutant General of the state in which the member served.

Selective Service Records.

Active-duty health records. Most of these records have not been retired to NPRC-MPR since the dates in the following chart. Those records are managed by the Department of Veterans Affairs, Records Management Center, 4360 Goodfellow Blvd., Bldg. 104, St. Louis, MO 63120-8950. Call the VA toll free number at 1-800-827-1000 to identify the current location of specific health records and to find out how to obtain releasable documents or information.

Branch	Status	Health Record to VA
Army	Discharged, retired, or separated from any component	Oct. 16, 1992
Air Force	Discharged, retired, or separated from active duty	May 1, 1994
	Discharged or retired from Reserves or National Guard	June 1, 1994
Navy	Discharged, retired, or separated from any component	Jan. 31, 1994
Marine Corps	Discharged, retired, or separated from any component	May 1, 1994
Coast Guard	Discharged, retired, or separated from active duty—Reservists with ninety days active duty for training	April 1, 1998

Source: www.archives.gove/st-louis/military-personnel

FAILURE TO CONSIDER ALL EVIDENCE IN A CLAIM FILE

Carefully screen the records used by the VA to adjudicate your claim. You want to be certain that all the evidence that substantiated your claim was considered. The RO may have passed over key pieces of evidence that led to the conclusion that the substantive evidence had no probative value. For example, if after obtaining a complete copy of your claim file you realize the history of military hospitalizations was overlooked, you have solid grounds to appeal your denial based on Clear and Unmistakable Error.

Also, when additional evidence is submitted with the formal appeal brief, you should receive an SSOC based on this new evidence. The letter should arrive in a timely manner. If it does not, contact the BVA and make sure that your appeal has been certified and that the VA has acknowledged receipt of the additional materials you submitted. Otherwise, you may have to wait as many as two years before a judge hears your appeal.

Finally, if you are a veteran whose MOS or AFSC is non-combat-related, your claim will most likely be denied. Unless you are able to prove that your injury or traumatic event was incurred in the service, the VA will be of little help to you. Action on your part is key because proving your claim is your responsibility, not the VA's.

Be proactive and track down evidence. You may have neglected evidence that could tip the scales in your favor. Evidence you need may be hiding in after-action reports, unit history records, sworn statements from fellow veterans, or your own sworn statement detailing the events and circumstances.

Incorrect Combat Information

Provide historical records, if necessary, to prove that you were in direct combat. These records can be significant, as shown in the case of a Korean War veteran who was denied service-connection benefits for a cold weather injury because his whereabouts in North Korea at the time of the war did not qualify as a combat zone. The VA argued that because his alleged combat in North Korea did not take place in the area of the Chosen Reservoir, he was not entitled to presumptive service connection for cold injuries as authorized under Title 38 USC §1154(a) and 38 CFR §3.303 and §3.304(d). The local RO held that because the veteran had not fought in the area of the Chosen Reservoir he had to provide evidence that showed he was in combat. Not only did he have to prove he was a combatant, but because his MOS was that of a signal corps technician assigned to a field artillery battalion, the local Regional Office also demanded he provide proof that he physically confronted the Chinese Army.

The veteran provided historical records that proved his unit's day-by-day march to Yalu River and the retreat back to the 38th Parallel was part of Eighth Army's first year of direct combat in Korea. However, VA Manual-21-1MR Part III Subpart iv, Chapter 4, Section E-21(b)(c)(e) and (f), stated that for a cold weather injury to qualify for direct service connection, the enemy had to be engaged in combat in the Chosen Reservoir area. The VA conceded that those individuals were exposed to severe cold weather (20 to 50 degrees F below zero). Fortunately for the veteran, when his appeal was heard before a BVA traveling judge, the Regional Office's decision was vacated and the judge granted benefits.

Neglecting to Recognize New Geography

Another reason to examine copies of your records and documents closely is to identify geographical changes, including renamed cities or countries or redrawn borders. An RO may overlook these alterations—an error that could be detrimental to your case. For example, a veteran's authorized representative confronted an RO who had denied the veteran's claim for Agent Orange because of a city name change. The veteran's claim for service connection had been denied because the veteran had supposedly not been stationed in Vietnam. However, the records showed that the veteran had been right outside Saigon. With this challenge to his decision, the RO pulled out a world atlas and, pointing to Vietnam, told the representative to show where Saigon was located. In disbelief, the representative pointed to Ho Chi Minh City and informed him that before the withdrawal of U.S. forces from Vietnam, the city was called Saigon. The RO refused to change his decision because his map clearly established there was no such city as Saigon. The issue was finally resolved when the dispute reached the RO's supervisor. If the alert representative had not realized the RO's oversight, the veteran would have had his claim denied and would have been forced into a prolonged appeal process.

Ignoring Probative Evidence

When a claim is denied, a copy of the rating decision will be attached to the denial letter. Be aware that the rating decision is required to include a written statement of the reasons or bases for the VA's findings and conclusions on all material issues of fact and law presented in the record. The statement must be adequate enough for an appellant to understand the precise basis for the decision, as well as to facilitate informed review in the CAVC. Ideally, in these statements VA adjudicators will discuss all the evidence on record, whether the evidence is persuasive or unpersuasive, and why in plain terms you are not entitled to benefits.

In reality, ROs spend very little time meticulously reviewing the Code of Federal Regulations to ensure you their decision is just and in accordance with the law.

CHANGING THE DEFINITION OF "COMBAT-RELATED"

Trauma Cases Surge Among Troops
By Pauline Jelinek, AP
Posted: 2008-05-28
Washington

The number of troops with new cases of post-traumatic stress disorder jumped by roughly 50 percent in 2007 amid the military buildup in Iraq and increased violence there and in Afghanistan.

Records show roughly 40,000 troops have been diagnosed with the illness, also known as PTSD, since 2003. Officials believe that many more are likely keeping their illness a secret.

More troops are serving multiple tours of duty in Iraq and Afghanistan, which may have contributed to

Throughout the years, thousands of veterans have not pursued an appeal simply because the veteran presumed that the VA carefully weighed all evidence and correctly and completely cited the Code of Federal Regulations as it applied to the veteran's claim. Again, having a copy of all the documents you send to the VA when submitting an appeal is imperative. If the adjudicators overlook evidence you submitted or spend too little time explaining a denial, you may raise those issues. Also, using statutes, regulations, and court decisions, the VA must justify in terms you and the Court can easily understand why you are not entitled.

the rise in reports of post-traumatic stress disorder, mental health experts suggested.

"I don't think right now we . . . have good numbers," Army Surgeon General Eric Schoomaker said Tuesday.

Defense officials had not previously disclosed the number of PTSD cases from Iraq and Afghanistan.

Army statistics showed there were nearly 14,000 newly diagnosed cases across the services in 2007 compared with more than 9,500 new cases the previous year and 1,632 in 2003.

Schoomaker attributed the big rise over the years partly to the fact that officials started an electronic record system in 2004 that captures more information, and to the fact that as time goes on the people keeping records are more knowledgeable about the illness.

He also blamed increased exposure of troops to combat.

continued on next page

continued from previous page

Factors increasing troop exposure to combat in 2007 included President Bush's troop buildup and the fact that 2007 was the most violent year in both conflicts.

More troops also were serving their second, third or fourth tours of duty—a factor mental health experts say dramatically increases stress. And in order to supply enough forces for the buildup, officials also extended tour lengths to 15 months from 12, another factor that caused extra emotional strain.

Officials have been encouraging troops to get help even if it means they go to civilian therapists and don't report it to the military.

"We're trying very hard to encourage soldiers and families to seek care and to not have them feel in any way, shape or form that we're looking over their shoulder or that we're invading their privacy," Schoomaker told a group of defense writers.

Noting that stigma is a problem in American civilian society, not just the military, he said, "I think that's the preferred way to do it."

The accounting of diagnosed cases released Tuesday shows those hardest hit last year were Marines and Army personnel, the two ground forces bearing the brunt of combat in Iraq and Afghanistan.

The Army reported more than 10,000 new cases last year, compared with more than 6,800 new cases the previous year. More than 28,000 soldiers altogether were diagnosed with the disorder over the last five years, the data showed.

The Marine Corps had more than 2,100 new cases in 2007, compared with 1,366 in 2006. More than 5,000

Marines have been diagnosed with PTSD since 2003, the data showed.

Navy officials who would have data on Marine health issues did not return a phone call seeking to confirm the numbers released by Schoomaker's office.

Schoomaker said he believes PTSD is widely misunderstood by the press and the public—and that what is often just normal post-traumatic anxiety and stress is mistaken for full-blown PTSD.

Experts say many troops have symptoms of stress, such as nightmares and flashbacks, and can get better with early treatment.

The Pentagon had previously only given a percentage of troops believed affected by depression, anxiety, stress and so on—saying up to 20 percent return home with symptoms of mental health problems. A recent private study estimated that could mean up to 300,000 of those who've served have symptoms.

The Veterans Affairs Department said recently it has seen some 120,000 Iraq and Afghanistan veterans who have received at least a preliminary mental health diagnosis, with PTSD being the most common diagnosis at nearly 60,000.

An undisclosed number of troops also go to private care providers who are part of the huge military health care system. Schoomaker noted that National Guard and Reserve troops often go home to communities where there is not a veterans facility nearby.

"We're working very hard with the VA and with the National Guard and Reserves to get a better feel for, a grasp on, how big this is," Schoomaker said, adding that

continued on next page

continued from previous page

over time officials will be able to collect data and get "a better feel for, handle on, the numbers." ●

Source: http://news.aol.com/story/_a/trauma-cases-surge-among-troops/20080528091409990001

FAILURE TO PROVIDE AN ACCURATE ADJUDICATION SYSTEM

Use of Medical Templates

The VA adjudication system uses medical templates in an attempt to lead the adjudicator to an objective decision based on the medical evidence of record. The major problem with this type of protocol is that the law and medicine are fluid and likely to change over time. Keeping the medical template current is not a priority for the VA.

Fewer Personnel Processing More Claims

During the Reagan administration, the Veterans Administration (as it was known then) reorganized the internal structure of the adjudication division in all fifty-seven Regional Offices. It replaced attorneys, physicians, and occupational specialists with nonspecialized adjudicators. The VA further authorized the practice of single signature rating decisions. As a result, pending claims began spiraling upward. In 2007, at an all-time high, it took an average of 183 days before a new claim began the rating process. Although the VA has claimed for the past decade that it is creating a new plan that will reduce the processing time and backlog of claims for compensation benefits, it has shown no signs of doing so. The closest the VA has come to achieving its goal of 125 days processing time was in 2004 when it reached a record low of 166 days.

Growing Backlog

By replacing attorneys, physicians, and occupational specialists with lay employees to decide these legal and medical issues, the VA removed more than nine hundred highly skilled professional positions at a great savings. This action enabled the Veterans Benefits Administration (VBA) to eliminate the salary expenses and employee benefits required for these three expensive professional groups. In today's job market, the VBA's downsizing of ROs shaved more than a hundred million dollars per year from the budget. Millions more are saved each year by permitting a single RO to decide the medical and legal issues of a claim that previously required the experience of three professionally trained specialists. Even more millions of dollars are saved annually because ROs—minimally trained in law and medicine—often underevaluate veterans' medical problems. A "Five Year Comparison of Combined Degree Service-Connected Disabilities for Veterans Who Began Receiving Compensation" between fiscal years 2001 and 2005 reported that 65 percent of the benefits granted during this period were rated between 0 and 30 percent. During the 2005 fiscal year, the group of veterans who were rated 10 percent disabled accounted for 51 percent within this group's total of 1,526,278 veterans. With a backlog of more than 400,000 new claims in 2007, these minimally qualified adjudicators are expected to increase production, which threatens the accuracy of decisions rendered by these adjudicators.

BACKLOG 2008
THE SIX MAJOR PROBLEM AREAS

Statement of Richard Paul Cohen, Executive Director, National Organization of Veterans' Advocates, Inc. (NOVA)

Before the Subcommittee on Disability Assistance and Memorial Affairs, VA Committee, U.S. House of Representatives

Regarding: VA's disability claims process at the Regional Office level, including what measures can be taken to improve its effectiveness in lessening the 600,000-plus claims backlog, and solutions for improving the VA claims process system in general.

Observations

Throughout 2007, top VA officials such as Daniel Cooper, VA's Veterans Benefits Administration Director, informed Congress about the backlog and excessive delays veterans are facing when filing a claim for VA benefits. Unfortunately, it is NOVA's conclusion that 2008 has brought little to no change in the following six major problem areas causing or contributing to the VA's inability to process a veteran's claim in a timely fashion. All of these problems require immediate attention and action in order for our nation's veterans to see any real improvement in a system upon which they rely for benefits and assistance.

(1) Backlog

In 2006, the backlog of claims for VA benefits, has skyrocketed to over 654,000 claims. At the same time, the VA received some 800,000 new claims in 2006, making it nearly impossible for VA staff to effectively address the 654,000 backlogged claims waiting to be processed and decided.

(2) Processing Time

When a veteran submits a new claim for VA benefits, he or she must currently wait an average of 177 days—almost six months—before getting the first decision. This six-month processing time consists primarily of the VA obtaining evidence, usually with the veteran's assistance. When the VA does finally issue a decision, it is not always favorable. When a veteran appeals an adverse decision, the processing time for a claim on appeal on average is 971 days (177 days for the initial processing of a new client plus 971 days for appeal to be ultimately adjudicated).

(3) Insufficient Staffing

As of April 30, 2007, the VBA had 12,684 employees processing veteran's claims. In September 2007, former VA Secretary Jim Nicholson reported that 1,100 new staff had been hired in an effort to reduce the 177 days it takes the VA to issue the first decision on a new claim. Even with these new hires, 13,784 VBA employees are being tasked with processing and deciding over 1.4 million new and backlogged claims.

continued on next page

continued from previous page

(4) Insufficient Training

In 2006, the VA's Office of Inspector General conducted a survey of Rating Veterans Service Representatives ("raters") and Decision Review Officers ("DROs"). The results of the survey revealed that within the last year they had received 10 hours or less of formal classroom instruction on rating policies and procedures. Given that the VA is the second largest government agency with 57 regional offices and over 12,000 staff throughout the country, 10 hours of training cannot possibly suffice to keep all of the VA's local offices and staff in step with all the policies and procedures directly affecting veterans' claims.

(5) Inappropriate Production Standards

Raters and DROs are held to production standards of completing decisions in three to five cases per day, which are tied to awards and bonuses and which adversely affect the quality of their work and the accuracy of their decisions. Nearly half (47%) of those surveyed said it was difficult or very difficult to meet their daily production standards. Forty-nine percent stated that they had difficulty meeting their production standards without sacrificing quality. And 57% stated they have difficulty meeting their production standards if they ensure that they have sufficient evidence for each rating and thoroughly review the evidence. These adjudicators are supposed to make decisions based on the evidence in the veteran's claims folder, which can be anywhere from a couple of hundred to several thousand pages of records. But, by forcing VA adjudicators to make three to five decisions per day, the decision maker is forced to make rush decisions, oftentimes without genuinely reviewing the veteran's entire claims file.

(6) Inaccurate, Inconsistent Decision Making

According to calculations derived from the Reports of the Chairman of the Board of Veterans' Appeals the accuracy rate in disability benefit decisions by the VA is less than 20%, rather than the 88% accuracy rate reported by the VA in 2006. The VA's Office of the Inspector General's 2006 survey revealed that 52.4% of Regional Office raters believed it was somewhat likely or very likely that two or more different ratings (one resulting in more compensation for the veteran) for the same medical condition could be supported.

In addition, veterans' advocates are now finding that VA rating officers and examiners are ignoring the diagnostic criteria contained in the *DSM* published by the American Psychiatric Association. Giving more weight to their personal biases than the diagnostic criteria, VA raters and examiners are denying PTSD claims submitted by combat veterans, falsely concluding that the veteran's combat stressor was insufficient for a diagnosis of PTSD. ●

Source: http://veterans.house.gov/hearings/hearing.aspx?NewsID=189

FAILURE TO MAINTAIN OBJECTIVITY

If your claim is denied, read the Rating Team member's rationale carefully and determine if the decision reflects the adjudicator's personal opinion or is based on the case's facts. If personal opinion played a role in the decision process, the adjudicator broke the law. Keep in mind, the majority of Rating Team members did not serve in the military. They are government employees and have no direct combat experience.

Before You File the Notice of Disagreement

- Obtain a copy of the actual examination report from the medical center where the exam was administered. By law, you cannot be denied a copy of the exam or any notes associated with the exam. The FOIA mandates the VA must comply with your request.

- Next, go to the VA's website where each examination is listed alphabetically and obtain a copy of the C&P Examination template used during your examination. Make copies of each exam that applies to you.

- Review the details of these examination reports to ensure they are in compliance with every medical template.

- Challenge any statements by the examiner that

are not based on an accepted medical principle. Findings based on a personal opinion are unacceptable.

- Take the C&P examiner's report along with a copy of the applicable medical template to your medical specialist and ask him or her to examine you based on the template. Ask the doctor to include in his or her report a rebuttal to any statement made by a VA examiner that is not based on accepted medical principles or facts.

- If you have not already done so, request a complete copy of your claim file from the Regional Office that is processing your claim. Remember, you cannot argue your case unless you know everything they know. Both the VBA and the Veterans Health Administration (VHA) are bound by the FOIA.

Armed with this information you can make a sound argument based on the actual facts of the case and show that the adjudicator and the C&P Examiner exercised their personal opinion and failed to follow the law or principles of medicine.

If you were denied service connection for an injury or illness because of a flawed C&P Examination less than a year after you filed your claim, file a NOD. If it has been more than a year, file an action to reopen your claim based on new and material evidence or a clear and unmistakable error.

FAILURE TO AUTHORIZE A SPECIALTY MEDICAL EXAMINATION

When we talk about the VBA and the VHA, we assume that the two VA agencies are working in total harmony with one another, with one common goal: to serve the veteran. Unfortunately, that is seldom the case. Each agency has its own interests that it must protect and promote. Each agency is responsible for its operational costs and is not obligated to tailor its operational needs to enhance the other's budget necessities.

How It Really Works

38 CFR Part 4 §4.2 Interpretation of Examination Report states, in part, "if a diagnosis is not supported by the findings on the examination report or if the report does not contain sufficient detail, it is incumbent upon the rating board to return the report as inadequate for evaluation purposes."

WHAT HAPPENS

Inadequate C&P Examination is submitted to the Regional Office ⇨

Regional Office forwards the C&P Examination to the Ratings Board ⇨

Ratings Board rejects the claim because the C&P Examination did not support the diagnosis ⇨

Regional Office denies claim benefits ●

However, the C&P Examination often does not return to the VA Medical Center because it was inadequate or the Medical Center failed to comply with the special instructions requested by the BVA. A common scenario is that the RO maintains you are not entitled to compensation benefits because the C&P Examination failed to medically substantiate the claim in the medical evaluation report. By accepting a flawed C&P Examination, the

---

WHAT SHOULD HAPPEN

Incomplete diagnosis submitted to the Regional Office⇨

Regional Office reviews the C&P Examination and finds inadequacies ⇨

Regional Office returns the C&P to the VA Medical Center, making sure that:

the medical examiner is a specialist who possesses the education needed to make an informed diagnosis

the medical examiner reviews the veteran's claim file before the examination

the medical examiner complies with 38 CFR § 3.159 (c)(4) and follows the correct protocol ⇨

Regional Office forwards the C&P Examination to the Ratings Board ⇨

Ratings Board accepts the claim because the C&P Examination supports the diagnosis ●

VA has practiced unfair adjudication that ultimately penalizes you.

ROs, Appeals Officers (AOs), and DROs are responsible to ensure that the C&P Examiners are in total compliance with VHA's manual, *VHA Handbook 1601E.01*. They also should ensure examinations are performed by specialists. Often, a medical person in the C&P unit examines the appellant. A "medical person" may be a nurse practitioner, a physician's assistant, a resident doctor from a university medical school, or even occasionally a physician who was assigned to the compensation unit but who is not necessarily qualified to conduct the specialist exams.

AOs have been known to ignore complaints from appellants saying their C&P Examinations were flawed. Veterans may complain that their examiners did not reviewed the claim file prior to examination or specifically failed to comply with 38 CFR §3.159 (c)(4) "VA duty to assist claimant in obtaining evidence" or follow the appropriate protocol as outlined by AMIE/CAPRI C&P Examination worksheets.

After the BVA judge reviews the file and finds the complaint has merits, your appeal is remanded to the Regional Office with instructions for a new C&P Examination to address the medical issues you have raised. The cycle starts again, and this time if the Regional Office does not grant the benefits it will likely be longer before the BVA judge reviews the file. It is entirely possible a situation like this could be repeated several more times before the issue is closed. In some cases, however, BVA judges have reversed the Regional Offices' decision and granted the benefits outright with instructions to start the entitlement process.

FAILURE TO REMOVE UNQUALIFIED ADJUDICATORS

There are reasons why management cannot and will not remove unqualified adjudicators from the system. Once an individual becomes a permanent employee under the Civil Service Personnel System, marginal performance is not grounds for dismissal. Because upward mobility is limited and severe ramifications for an average performance are not in place, an adjudicator may have little incentive to perform up to his or her highest standard.

What Can Be Done

VA staff must be regularly and effectively trained. One solution is periodic (quarterly or semi-annual) training in VA law and medicine for raters, DROs, and Regional Office staff. This needs to include a review of important opinions from the U.S. Court of Appeals for Veterans Claims and application of them where relevant. Key court cases should be sent to VA adjudicators on a timely basis so they can follow and apply Court of Appeals for Veteran Claims precedent to their current cases. Review of medical protocol and examination regulations should be mandatory for clinicians who conduct psychological evaluations and C&P Examinations.

Staff should also be refreshed on the meaning of the Duty to Assist as well as notification of veterans, regulations regarding the benefit of the doubt, and how to rate difficult medical conditions. Increasing VA staff is not effective unless adequate education and training is provided.

What This Means to You

Ask the RO

- What training does the adjudicator who will be hearing my appeal have?
- What recent cases are similar to mine and what was outcome?
- What recent cases similar to mine were denied and what were the reasons for denial?

No Tracking of Reversals

Management does not examine the adjudicator's performance by the number of adjudicated claims that were appealed by veterans. When the BVA remands appeals to the Regional Office for lack of proper development, for failure to apply the law correctly, or for accepting flawed C&P Examinations as a basis for denial of compensation benefits, particular staff members are not held accountable as the weakest link in the process.

What Can Be Done

The VA should be required to maintain statistics on the Regional Office denial rate. Without statistics on the RO's denial rate, it is impossible to determine how many claimants abandon their claims rather than proceed with an appeal. Also, if denial rates are broken down by type of claim, this would provide understanding of the examiner's and rater's experiences in dealing with various claims.

What This Means to You

Ask the RO

- What is the percentage of appeals that are granted benefits for cases like yours?
- Why were the denied claims denied?

Tracking Only Closed Claims

The undersecretaries' and deputy undersecretaries' interest is in the number of claims that are closed. In fiscal years 2003 and 2004, the VA stated that it processed 1.5 million claims of which it proudly announced it added more than 300,000 veterans to the rolls. However, what the department did not make available was the number of claims that were denied out of the remaining 1.2 million processed claims. So, you could surmise that an adjudicator who rates a claim can safely deny it without fear of being criticized or punished monetarily. From a management point of view, he or she is a good team player.

What Can Be Done

Adjudications should concentrate on accuracy, not simply speed or the number of cases closed. Although every claimant wants a speedy decision, a hasty and erroneous decision will not help you. The time spent providing an accurate and just rating will reduce the VA's need for repeated reviews of the same claim. Veterans then are forced to appeal. By encouraging VA adjudicators to make quality decisions (as opposed to meeting a quota of decisions per day), every veteran's entire claims folder can be reviewed thoroughly in regard to VA law, regulations, and case law.

What This Means to You

Ask the RO

- How many staff members are currently handling claims in this office?
- How many cases does each staff member handle at one time?

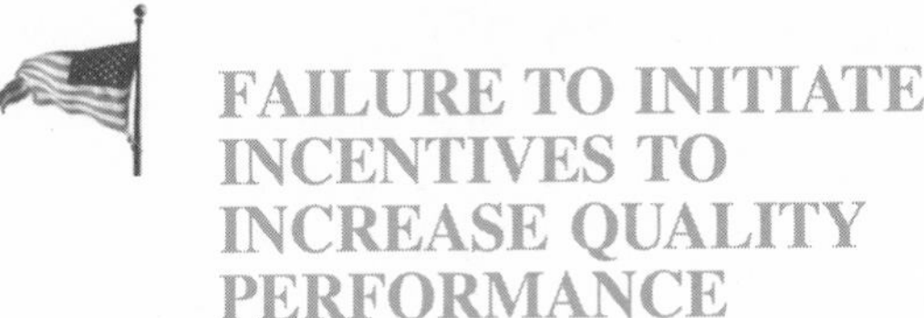

FAILURE TO INITIATE INCENTIVES TO INCREASE QUALITY PERFORMANCE

Awarding Bonuses to Senior Officials in Spite of Their Performances

The VA battles criticism by declaring its award process is "necessary to attract and retain hardworking senior employees." Why would anyone appointed by the Secretary of the Department of Veterans Affairs want to sit on the board that recommends performance bonuses for senior officials? The answer is behind door number three: twenty-one of thirty-two members on the bonus review board approved bonuses that directly affected them. An Associated Press article noted that the average bonus was more than $16,000 for these political appointees and undersecretaries.

These end-of-the-year bonuses were justified by the extraordinary performance of undersecretaries and deputy undersecretaries in 2006. These honorariums cost the taxpayers more than $3.8 million. In one case, the Associated Press documented that a deputy undersecretary and his wife, who was a VA director, received a combined gift of $42,000. This deputy undersecretary sat on two of the bonus review boards.

Keep in mind that one of the winners was the undersecretary for benefits who manages a division that is supposed to reduce the backlog of nearly 400,000 pending claims. However, under his direction, the number of backlogged claims continued to increase. According to the bonus review board, his contributions merited a bonus.

Another official honored for his performance was an undersecretary in the VHA whose budgetary skills shortchanged veterans' health care by $1.3 billion in 2006. In an eleventh-hour reprieve, Congress authorized the immediate release of funds for veterans in need of health care.

This entire award process initiates what might be called a "trickle down supremacy policy," whereby a monetary reward is the leverage that moves less senior officials to carry out orders from the White House and the Office of Management and Budget (OMB). Let's theorize how this might work. A meeting with the president, director of the OMB, and the secretary of the VA to discuss how they will trim the VA budget is necessary. They must then also take into account the reaction of veterans organizations, news media, the majority of the Congress, and the enormous veteran population. Their outrage over a slimmer budget would seriously affect the recruitment for an all-volunteer military system.

Meeting Budgetary Goals

Here are some ways that have proved successful for past administrations that have allowed them to meet their budget without losing the support of veterans:

- Removing attorneys, physicians, and occupation specialists from rating boards and replacing them with untrained adjudicators who were given single signature rating authority. (See pp. 86–87.)

- Introducing a nationwide hospital-bed downsizing program. From the mid-1980s to the mid-1990s, administrations were able to shave billions off the budget through this implementation. Savings resulted from eliminating expensive medical staffing and support personnel. The program was sold on the basis that the savings would be used to build nursing homes for the older veterans and reach out to distant communities to provide medical care for veterans within the Medical Center's region of responsibility.

- Treating only veterans with service-connected injuries and illnesses owing to the shortage of key medical staff. A priority group system was devised whereby veterans were placed in one of eight categories (see chart on pp. 103–105). Veterans in the first group received treatment for any medical problem if they were rated 50 percent or more disabled. On the other end of the spectrum was the veteran whose income factors into the eligibility prerequisites for treatment. Within this group, veterans were charged a copayment for services rendered, and their health insurance or Medicare was billed for these medical services.

- Not treating veterans over a certain age for particular ailments because of the medical expense and time required. In 2005 VA Medical Center Bay Pines Florida issued a new policy order for all primary care physicians related to standard laboratory orders. Again the VHA used its management style of grouping services

VA HEALTH CARE

Fact Sheet 164-2
March 2008

ENROLLMENT PRIORITY GROUPS

Priority Group	Definition
1	• Veterans with VA-rated service-connected disabilities 50% or more disabling • Veterans determined by VA to be unemployable owing to service-connected conditions
2	• Veterans with VA-rated service-connected disabilities 30% or 40% disabling
3	• Veterans who are Former Prisoners of War (POWs) • Veterans awarded a Purple Heart medal • Veterans whose discharge was for a disability that was incurred or aggravated in the line of duty • Veterans with VA-rated service-connected disabilities 10% or 20% disabling • Veterans awarded special eligibility classification under *Title 38, USC, Section 1151*, "benefits for individuals disabled by treatment or vocational rehabilitation"
4	• Veterans who are receiving aid and attendance or housebound benefits from VA • Veterans who have been determined by VA to be catastrophically disabled
5	• Nonservice-connected veterans and noncompensable service-connected veterans rated as 0% disabled by VA and whose annual income and net worth are below the VA national income threshold • Veterans receiving VA pension benefits • Veterans eligible for Medicaid programs

continued on next page

according to specific standards. In this case, veterans were grouped according to whether they were male and female and by age groups between fifty-two and eighty and over eighty years old. In the male grouping, if a veteran was eighty or older, they terminated the prostate cancer test (PSA) even if the physician suspected the veteran might have prostate cancer. An article appearing in the *Journal of the American Medical Association* indicated that ordering PSA tests for elderly male patients seventy years or older was a questionable

continued from previous page

Priority Group	Definition
6	• World War I veterans • Compensable 0 percent service-connected veterans • Veterans exposed to ionizing radiation during atmospheric testing or during the occupation of Hiroshima and Nagasaki • Project 112/SHAD participants • Veterans who served in a theater of combat operations after November 11, 1998 as follows: ▸ Veterans discharged from active duty on or after January 28, 2003, who were enrolled as of January 28, 2008, and veterans who apply for enrollment after January 28, 2008, for five years post discharge ▸ Veterans discharged from active duty before January 28, 2003, who apply for enrollment after January 28, 2008, until January 27, 2011
7	• Veterans with income and/or net worth above the VA national income threshold and income below the geographic income threshold who agree to pay copays

policy. The article argued that prostate cancer is a slow-moving cause of death and the veteran could easily die from other causes before the cancer became terminal. With the medical profession leaning toward less or no PSA testing in male patients seventy years or older, the VA Hospital Administration quickly concluded this was a great way to cut money out of the budget. A GAO study in 2000 pointed out that the VA hospitals and clinics saw more than four million patients a year. If they saved at least five dollars per test and they tested only two hundred

8	• Veterans with income and/or net worth above the VA national income threshold and the geographic income threshold who agree to pay copays ▸ Subpriority a: Noncompensable 0% service-connected veterans enrolled as of January 16, 2003, and who have remained enrolled since that date ▸ Subpriority c: Nonservice-connected veterans enrolled as of January 16, 2003, and who have remained enrolled since that date ▸ Subpriority e*: Noncompensable 0% service-connected veterans applying for enrollment after January 16, 2003 ▸ Subpriority g*: Nonservice-connected veterans applying for enrollment after January 16, 2003

***Note:** Veterans assigned to Priority Groups 8e or 8g are not eligible for enrollment as a result of the enrollment restriction, which suspended enrolling new high-income veterans who apply for care after January 16, 2003. Veterans enrolled in Priority Groups 8a or 8c remain enrolled and eligible for the full-range of VA health care benefits.

Source: http://www.va.gov/healtheligibility/Library/pubs/EPG/EnrollmentPriorityGroups.pdf

thousand veterans in this age group, they could trim the budget by one million dollars per year.

- Limiting the time an examiner can spend evaluating your illness or injury. At Bay Pines Medical Center in St. Petersburg, Florida, this policy is in full swing. A psychologist who refused to go along with this policy on the grounds that he could not adequately evaluate the seriousness of a veteran's mental health problem was fired. He contended that ninety minutes to review VA and service records and prepare a comprehensive report was not adequate. The psychologist's case was finally heard by the U.S. Merit Systems Protection Board, which reinstated him. However, he was transferred out of the C&P Evaluation unit for failure to be a team player.

Savings When Denying a Claim

Never forget the fact that every time a claim is denied for veterans' benefits, the VA saves money. When multiplied over the lifetime of a veteran the amount of savings could be substantial. To illustrate, let's say a thirty-five-year-old veteran has been awarded a 10 percent disability rating. His life expectancy is eighty years, which means he will receive compensation benefits for the next forty-five years. This equates to $63,180 without considering the annual cost of living added to his monthly award or the cost of medical care over the next forty-five years.

Even worse is that many veterans, especially older ones, will die before their claims are resolved. That fact alone saves the VA millions of dollars every year.

The United States has been denying its veterans benefits in order to save money since the Revolutionary War era. To encourage the wealthy to lend more money to the Continental Congress and to gain the support of military officers, Gouverneur Morris of Pennsylvania pushed a bill through the congress that gave military officers half-pay for life if they continued fighting until the end of the war. His proposal ignored the enlisted ranks who were fighting without pay and who were suffering and dying in the cold. On January 1, 1791, the enlisted ranks of Pennsylvania killed one of their captains and wounded other officers, immobilizing the troops so that they could march to Philadelphia to demand pay. The congress capitulated to their demands and granted back pay.

The Veterans Act of 1924 extended service-connected benefits to any veterans of World War I who suffered additional injuries or disabilities while hospitalized by the VA. The statute, known as Section 213 Benefits, entitled veterans to compensation benefits whether the additional injuries or disabilities were the result of hospital staff negligence or not.

A decade later, in 1934, at the urging of the Franklin D. Roosevelt administration and without congressional backing, the VA changed the language of the regulation to make benefits payable only when negligence could be proved. This measure was taken to reduce the financial drain caused by providing support to veterans during the Great Depression, but it remained in place for the next seventy-four years, until a veteran named Fred P. Gardner took the issue to the Supreme Court.

PART 3

BUILDING A HEARING BOOK

You and your representative are waiting to be called into the hearing room. It is a time of high anxiety. The unknown awaits you. Your confidence is bouncing back and forth between "I know all the facts to support why I should be entitled to benefits" to "Because I am nervous, I will forget the facts and present statements based on my opinion rather than the evidence of the case."

Think of your hearing as if it were a baseball game. It is the bottom of the ninth inning, the bases are loaded, you're at bat, and you need a home run to win the game. Your *hearing book* is the bat that will let you knock the ball out of the park.

Remember this: give the hearing judge *reasons* to grant the benefits. Your arguments must convince the judge that your appeal is grantable because it is factually correct and in compliance with all regulations, statutes, and court decisions. At this stage, you are in an adversarial dispute with the Regional Office. Your arguments cannot be built on personal opinions. As they used to say in the 1950s TV show *Dragnet*, "just the facts, sir, just the facts." To stay focused on the facts you must build a hearing book.

THE HEARING BOOK

There is nothing carved in stone that dictates how a hearing book should be prepared. You cannot say one format or outline will work for every appeal. What might work for you may not work for another appellant. What is important is that you organize your presentation in a way that allows you to cover all the issues, backed by hard evidence, quickly and succinctly.

A simple, inexpensive way to prepare a hearing book is to use a multipage fixed file folder or three-ring binder with dividers or tabbed inserts to separate various sections and documents. If you use a fixed file folder, you will need a two-hole punch to secure all statements and documents in chronological order. The size of the hearing book will depend on the number of issues being appealed and the amount of evidence you want the hearing judge to consider. It may be necessary to have more than one fixed file folder or loose-leaf binder. If this is the case, you want to make every file folder or notebook the same size and color. It is important to attach to the cover of the file folder or binder a cover sheet that clearly identifies the contents and indicates which volume it is. The last thing you want is to suddenly panic during the hearing because you cannot find a piece of evidence to support your argument.

The best way to set up a hearing book is first to create a table of contents identifying each section and subsection. Some common headings to organize your documents and arguments are cover page, table of contents, table of authorities, introduction, statement of historical facts, issues on appeal, discussion of each issue, and summary.

Below each of these components of the hearing book is discussed.

A typical cover page for a hearing book looks like this:

Board of Veterans Appeals
Washington, D.C., VA Regional Office
810 Vermont Avenue
Washington, DC 20420

James R. Rogers, Appellant. v. Washington, D.C., Regional Office POST4/TMN	VA Claim Number: CSS 112-22-5555 VBA Docket No. 06-99990

Initial Hearing Brief of the Appellant

JAMES R. ROGERS
4500 IAMVET Street
Washington, DC 20420
Telephone: 700-555-0000
E-Mail: Jrogers01@Yahoo.net

Volume 1 of 2

TABLE OF CONTENTS

A table of contents serves three purposes: it is a complete outline of your appeal, it will focus the hearing judge's attention on all the issues under appeal without requiring him or her to search through hundreds of documents to verify your arguments, and it requires the judge to detail every issue he or she rebuts. Here is an example:

Table of Contents page ii

continued on next page

continued from previous page

ISSUE VIII. 15

The appellant cited *Caluza v. Brown* 7 Vet.App. at 506 (1995) as a case in point that mandates presumptive service connection presumed as having an etiological nexus to military service by virtue of established facts relating to the time, location, and nature of a veteran's military service.

ISSUE IX. 16

Even if the decision is not found to be clearly erroneous, the decision should be reversed because Appeals Officers (AO) failed to give the appellant the benefit of the doubt as required.

SUMMARY 17

TABLE OF AUTHORITIES

A table of authorities is a table of contents for the legal documents used to argue your appeal. It is a list of legal references to other court cases, statutes, rules, citations, regulations, and amendments that support the arguments referenced in your Substantive Appeal.

You want to make known to the hearing judge exactly what case law, statutes, and regulations support your arguments. Here again, if the judge does not agree with your premise that these laws, regulation, and statutes apply to you, he or she must specifically state why they are not applicable. If you show in your written presentation why these laws, regulations, and statutes are applicable, you give the judge a reason to grant the benefit.

Here is an example:

Court of Appeals for Veterans Claims

Skyler v. Brown, 5 Vet.App. 146 (1993)
Irby v. Brown, 6 Vet.App. 132 (1994)
Caffrey v. Brown, 6 Vet.App. 377 (1994)
Peters v. Brown, 6 Vet.App. 540 (1994)
Willis v. Derwinski, 1 Vet.App. 63 (1991)
Wilson v. Derwinski, 1 Vet.App. 139 (1991)
Townsend v. Derwinski, 1 Vet.App. 408 (1991)

Code of Federal Regulations

38 CFR §3.103
Procedural due process and appellate rights
38 CFR §3.159
Department of Veterans Affairs assistance in developing claims

38 CFR §3.303 (b)
Principles relating to service connection
38 CFR §3.321 (b) (1)
General rating considerations
38 CFR §3.309
Disease subject to presumptive service connection

Case Law by Subject

Following is a list of case law as it pertains to various subjects you may be including in your appeal:

Agent Orange

Collette v. Brown, 95-7043 (1996)
McCay v. Brown, 9 Vet.App. 183 (1996)

Abandoned claim

Hyson v. Brown, 5 Vet.App. 262 (1993)

Arbitrary and capricious

Bailey v. Derwinski, 1 Vet.App. 441 (1991)
Butts v. Brown, 5 Vet.App. 532 (1993)
Ternus III v. Brown, 6 Vet.App. 370 (1994)
Venerson v. West, 12 Vet.App. 254 (1999)

Articulating reasons or bases

Caluza v. Brown, 7 Vet.App. 498 (1995)
Douglas v. Derwinski, 2 Vet.App. 435 (1992)
Gilbert v. Derwinski, 1 Vet.App. 49 (1990)
Hatlestas v. Derwinski, 1 Vet.App. 164 (1991)
Lathan v. Brown, 7 Vet.App. 359 (1995)
Murphy v. Derwinski, 1 Vet.App. 78 (1992)
O'Hare v. Derwinski, 1 Vet.App. 365 (1991)

Trytek v. Derwinski, 3 Vet.App. 153 (1992)

Benefit of the doubt

Gilbert v. Derwinski, 1 Vet.App. 49 (1990)
Willis v. Derwinski, 1 Vet.App. 63 (1990)

Burden of proof responsibility of veteran

Murphy v. Derwinski, 1 Vet.App. 78 (1992)

BVA failed to discuss evidence

Frankel v. Derwinski, 1 Vet.App. 23, 25-26 (1990)

BVA must review all issues reasonably raised

Fanning v. Brown, 4 Vet.App. 225 (1993)

Chronic diseases

Collette v. Brown, 95-7043 (1996)

Claims deemed abandoned

Ford v. Gober, 10 Vet.App. 531, 535 (1997)
Grivois v. Brown, 6 Vet.App. 136, 138 (1994)

Clear and unmistakable error (CUE)

Counts v. Brown, 6 Vet.App. 480 (1994)
Godwin v. Derwinski, 1 Vet.App. 419, 425 (1991)
Morgan v. Brown, 9 Vet.App. 161 (1996)
Porter v. Brown, 5 Vet.App. 233 (1993)
Russell v. Brown, 3 Vet.App. 134 (1992)
Weggenmann v. Brown, 5 Vet.App. 281 (1993)
Willis v. Derwinski, 1 Vet.App. 66 (1990)

Clearly erroneous finding of facts

Gilbert v. Derwinski, 1 Vet.App. 49, 57 (1990)

Porter v. Brown, 5 Vet.App. 233 (1993)

Combat status

Cohen v. Brown, 10 Vet.App. 128 (1997)
Collette v. Brown, 82F.3d.389 (1996)
Dizoglio v. Brown, 9 Vet.App. 163 (1996)
Moreau v. Brown, 9 Vet.App. 389 (1996)
Murillo v. Brown, 9 Vet.App. 322 (1996)
Thomas v. Brown, 10 Vet.App. 128, 138 (1997)

Continuity of symptomatology

Collette v. Brown, 95-7043 (1996)

Dependency and indemnity claim

Owings v. Brown, 8 Vet.App. 17 (1995)

Disability rating

Belin v. Derwinski, 2 Vet.App. 271 (1992)
Dofflemyers v. Derwinski, 2 Vet.App. 277, 280 (1992)
Gleicher v. Derwinski, 2 Vet.App. 26 (1991)
Holo v. Derwinski, 2 Vet.App. 169, 172 (1992)
Moyer v. Derwinski, 2 Vet.App. 289 (1992)
Sawyer v. Derwinski, 1 Vet.App. 130, 134-135 (1991)

Duty to assess credibility and weight of evidence

Wood v. Derwinski, 1 Vet.App. 190, 193 (1991)

Duty to assist

Ardison v. Brown, 6 Vet.App. 405 (1993)
Azurin v. Derwinski, 2 Vet.App. 489 (1992)
Connolly v. Derwinski, 1 Vet.App. 566 (1991)
Godwin v. Derwinski, 1 Vet.App. 419, 425 (1991)
Ivey v. Derwinski, 2 Vet.App. 320 (199)

Lathan v. Brown, 7 Vet.App. 359 (1995)
Murphy v. Derwinski, 1 Vet.App. 78 (1992)
Owings v. Brown, 8 Vet.App. 17 (1995)
Proscelle v. Derwinski, 2 Vet.App. 629 (1992)
Robinette v. Brown, 8 Vet.App. 69 (1995)
Weggenmann v. Brown, 5 Vet.App. 281 (1993)

Effective date

Evans v. West, 12 Vet.App. 396 (1999)
Jones v. West, 12 Vet.App. 98 (1999)
KL v. Brown, 5 Vet.App. 205 (1993)
Lapier v. Brown, 5 Vet.App. 215 (1993)
Padget v. Brown, 4 Vet.App. 247 (1993)
Perry v. West, 12 Vet.App. 365 (1999)
Quarles v. Derwinski, 3 Vet.App. (1993)
Servello v. Derwinski, 3 Vet.App. 196 (1992)
Swanson v. West, 12 Vet.App. 442 (1999)

Erroneous decisions

Basillote v. Derwinski, 3 Vet.App. 43 (1992)
Cahall v. Derwinski, 3 Vet.App. 4 (1991)
Cosman v. Principi, 3 Vet.App. 503 (1992)
Crandell v. Derwinski, 3 Vet.App. 33 (1992)
Fenderson v. West, 12 Vet.App. 119 (1999)
Gooden v. Derwinski, 3 Vet.App. 10 (1991)
Harder v. Brown, 5 Vet.App. 183 (1993)
Hohol v. Derwinski, 2 Vet.App. 169 (1992)
Houston v. Brown, 5 Vet.App. 245 (1993)
Jeffers v. Derwinski, 3 Vet.App. 22 (1991)
Nixon v. Derwinski, 3 Vet.App. 151 (1992)
Pond v. West, 12 Vet.App. 341 (1999)
Sanders v. Derwinski, 3 Vet.App. 334 (1992)
Woods v. Derwinski, 3 Vet.App. 376 (1992)

YR v. West, 11 Vet.App. 393 (1998)

Evidence is not limited

Douglas v. Derwinski, 2 Vet.App. 435 (1992)

Failed to advise veteran of all benefits he/she may be entitled to

Douglas v. Derwinski, 2 Vet.App. 435 (1992)

Failed to advise veteran of evidence necessary to complete claim

Robinette v. Brown, 8 Vet.App. 69 (1995)

Failed to apply the law

Johnson v. Brown, 9 Vet.App. 7, 10 (1996)

Failed to consider medical evidence of record

Frankel v. Derwinski, 1 Vet.App. 23, 25–26 (1990)

Failed to provide an adequate statement of reasons for decision

Allday v. Brown, 7 Vet.App. 517, 527 (1995)
Gilbert v. Derwinski, 1 Vet.App. 49, 57 (1990)
Johnston (Robert) v. Brown, 10 Vet.App. 80, 86 (1997)
Manibog v. Brown, 8 Vet.App. 465, 466 (1996)
McGinty v. Brown, 4 Vet.App. 428, 432–33 (1993)
Watson v. Brown, 4 Vet.App. 309, 315 (1993)

Failed to submit current medical examination

Dusek v. Derwinski, 2 Vet.App. 519 (1992)

Increased rating

Weggenmann v. Brown, 5 Vet.App. 281 (1993)

Individual unemployability

Fanning v. Brown, 4 Vet.App. 225 (1993)
Fluharty v. Derwinski, 2 Vet.App. 409 (1992)
Hatlestas v. Derwinski, 1 Vet.App. 164 (1991)
Moore v. Derwinski, 2 Vet.App. 67 (1992)
Proscelle v. Derwinski, 2 Vet.App. 629 (1992)

Issues not raised in the appellant's brief are deemed abandoned

Bucklinger v. Brown, 5 Vet.App. 435, 436 (1993)
Colvin v. Derwinski, 1 Vet.App. 171, 175 (1991)
Ford v. Gober, 10 Vet.App. 531, 535 (1997)
Gleicher v. Derwinski, 2 Vet.App. 26, 28 (1991)
Willis v. Derwinski, 1 Vet.App. 66, 70 (1991)

Lay Evidence

Brammer v. Derwinski, 3 Vet.App. 223 (1994)
Cahall v. Derwinski, 3 Vet.App. 4 (1991)
Caluza v. Brown, 7 Vet.App. 498 (1995)
Franko v. Brown, 4 Vet.App. 502 (1993)
Grottveit v. Brown, 5 Vet.App. 91 (1992)
Jeffers v. Derwinski, 3 Vet.App. 22 (1991)
Robinette v. Brown, 8 Vet.App. 69 (1995)
Smith v. Derwinski, 2 Vet.App. 137 (1992)

Medical evidence must be plausible or possible

Caluza v. Brown, 7 Vet.App. 498 (1995)
Grottveit v. Brown, 5 Vet.App. 91 (1992)
Lathan v. Brown, 7 Vet.App. 359 (1995)
Murphy v. Derwinski, 1 Vet.App. 78 (1992)
Proscelle v. Derwinski, 2 Vet.App. 629 (1992)
Robinette v. Brown, 8 Vet.App. 69 (1995)
Tirpak v. Derwinski, 2 Vet.App. 609 (1991)

Medical evidence must exist for current medical problem

Rabideau v. Derwinski, 2 Vet.App. 141 (1992)

Medical opinion

Hicks v. Brown, 8 Vet.App. 417 (1995)
Pond v. West, 12 Vet.App. 341 (1999)

Medical records alone not required to establish service connection

Ivey v. Derwinski, 2 Vet.App. 320 (1992)

Medical treatise

Wallin v. West, 11 Vet.App. 509 (1998)

New and material evidence

Brammer v. Derwinski, 3 Vet.App. 223 (1991)
Cartright v. Derwinski, 2 Vet.App. 24 (1991)
Counts v. Brown, 6 Vet.App. 473 (1994)
Cox v. Principi, 5 Vet.App. 95, 98 (1993)
Elkins v. West, 12 Vet.App. 209 (1999)
Jones v. Derwinski, 1 Vet.App. 213 (1991)
Justus v. Principi, 3 Vet.App. 510, 513 (1992)
King v. Brown, 5 Vet.App. 19 (1993)
Lind v. Principi, 3 Vet.App. 510 (1992)
Masors v. Derwinski, 2 Vet.App. 181, 185 (1992)
Paller V. Principi, 3 Vet.App. 535 (1992)
Robinette v. Brown, 8 Vet.App. 69 (1995)
Sklar v. Brown, 5 Vet.App. 140 (1993)

Nexus must exist between service and post-service

Rabideau v. Derwinski, 2 Vet.App. 141 (1992)

No plausible bases for decision

Ardison v. Brown, 6 Vet.App. 405 (1994)

Notice of Disagreement

Buckley v. West, 12 Vet.App. 76 (1998)
Magula v. Derwinski, 1 Vet.App. 76 (1990)
Whitt v. Derwinski, 1 Vet.App. 40 (1990)

Payment of unauthorized medical expenses

Paris, Appellant, v. Brown, 5 Vet.App. 75 (1993)

Post-traumatic Stress Disorder (PTSD)

Cosman v. Principi, 3 Vet.App. 503 (1992)
Crandell v. Derwinski, 3 Vet.App. 33 (1992)
Mitchem v. Brown, 9 Vet.App. 138 (1996)
Moreau v. Brown, 9 Vet.App. 389 (1996)
Murillo v. Brown, 9 Vet.App. 322 (1996)
Patton v. West, 12 Vet.App. 272 (1999)
Richard v. Brown, 9 Vet.App. 266 (1996)
Swan v. Brown, 5 Vet.App. 229 (1993)
Trytek v. Derwinski, 3 Vet.App. 153 (1992)
Wood v. Derwinski, 1 Vet.App. 406 (1991)
YR v. West, 11 Vet.App. 393 (1998)

Preexisting injury or disease

Collette v. Brown, 95-7043 (1996)

Prejudicial decision

Buckley v. West, 12 Vet.App. 76 (1998)

Probative and creditability of evidence

O'Hare v. Derwinski, 1 Vet.App. 365 (1991)

Proof of current disability

Brammer v. Derwinski, 3 Vet.App. 223 (1994)

Proof injury or illness occurred in service

Collette v. Brown, 95-7043 (1996)
Hayes v. Brown, 5 Vet.App. 60 (1993)

Reasons for rejecting any evidence favorable to the veteran

Gabrielson v. Brown, 7 Vet.App. 36, 39-40 (1994)
Gilbert v. Derwinski, 1 Vet.App. 49 (1990)

Reduction of rating

Karnas v. Derwinski, 1 Vet.App. 308 (1991)
Lehman v. Derwinski, 1 Vet.App. 339 (1991)

Relied on VA's own medical judgment

Chestnut v. Derwinski, 2 Vet.App. 613 (1992)

Remands

Ferguson v. Derwinski, 1 Vet.App. 428 (1991)
Gutierrez v. Principi, 19 Vet.App. 10 (2004)
Tucker v. West, 11 Vet.App. 369, 374 (1998)
Willis v. Derwinski, 1 Vet.App. 63 (1991)

Reopened Claim

Abernathy v. Derwinski, 2 Vet.App. 358 (1992)
Case v. Derwinski, 2 Vet.App. 592 (1992)
Colvin v. Derwinski, 1 Vet.App. 174 (1991)
Falzone v. Brown, 8 Vet.App. 398 (1995)
Giglio v. Derwinski, 2 Vet.App. 560 (1992)
Martinez v. Brown, 6 Vet.App. 462 (1994)
Miller v. Derwinski, 3 Vet.App. 90 (1992)
Mohr v. Derwinski, 3 Vet.App. 63 (1992)

Quinn v. Derwinski, 3 Vet.App. 23 (1992)
Sklar v. Brown, 5 Vet.App. 140 (1993)
Tablazon v. Brown, 8 Vet.App. 359 (1995)
Townsend v. Derwinski, 1 Vet.App. 408 (1991)
Tozian v. Derwinski, 3 Vet.App. 268 (1992)
Woods v. Derwinski, 3 Vet.App. 376 (1992)

Retroactivity of rating

Myler v. Derwinski, 1 Vet.App. 571 (1991)

Secondary medical condition

Buckley v. West, 12 Vet.App. 76 (1998)

Service connection

Garrett v. Derwinski, 2 Vet.App. 334 (1992)
*Wikman v. Derwinsk*i, 2 Vet.App. 272 (1992)

Sworn statements/testimony

Clouatre v. Derwinski, 3 Vet.App. 127 (1992)
Cuevas v. Principi, 3 Vet.App. 542 (1992)

Thorough and contemporaneous examination

Caffrey v. Brown, 6 Vet.App. 377 (1994)
Irby v. Brown, 6 Vet.App. 132 (1994)
Milostan v. Brown, 4 Vet.App. 250 (1993)
Skyler v. Brown, 5 Vet.App. 146 (1993)
Stegall v. West, 11 Vet.App. 268 (1998)

Total disability

Hersey v. Derwinski, 2 Vet.App. 91 (1992)

Unemployability TDIU rating

Cleary v. Principi, 3 Vet.App. 495 (1992)
Cox v. Principi, 5 Vet.App. 95, 98 (1993)

Moore v. Derwinski, 1 Vet.App. 83 (1990)
Norris v. West, 12 Vet.App. 413 (1999)
Proscelle v. Derwinski, 1 Vet.App. 629, 633–634 (1992)
Romeo v. Brown, 5 Vet.App. 388, 396 (1993)
Sanders v. Derwinski, 3 Vet.App. 334 (1992)
Wade v. Derwinski, 3 Vet.App. 70 (1992)

Unlawful act not to follow VA's regulations
Browder v. Derwinski, 1 Vet.App. 204, 205 (1991)

VA cannot reduce rating without evidenciary support
Karnas v. Derwinski, 1 Vet.App. 308 (1) (1991)

VA cannot ignore its own regulations
Fanning v. Brown, 4 Vet.App. 225 (1993)

VA cannot substitute its own medical judgment
Townsend v. Derwinski, 1 Vet.App. 408 (1991)
Willis v. Derwinski, 1 Vet.App. 66 (1990)

VA must acknowledge and consider all potentially relevant speculations
Lathan v. Brown, 7 Vet.App. 359 (1995)

VA must comply with mandate from court
Moore v. Derwinski, 2 Vet.App. 67 (1992)

VA must obtain C&P Examination
Proscelle v. Derwinski, 2 Vet.App. 629 (1992)

When reversal is appropriate
Gutierrez v. Principi, 19 Vet.App. 1, 10 (2004)

Johnson v. Brown, 9 Vet.App. 7, 10 (1996)
Lehman v. Derwinski, 1 Vet.App. 339, 343 (1991)

Where the Board fails to fulfill its duty

Browder v. Brown, 5 Vet.App. 268, 272 (1993)
Meeks v. Brown, 5 Vet.App. 284, 288 (1993)

INTRODUCTION

Your opening remarks should be a brief introduction that focuses on why the VA Rating Officer erred. Identify all the named individuals within the VA system that contributed to the denial of benefits and how the hearing judge will identify any new evidence that was not previously considered. Here is an example:

> **Introduction**
> Having been duly sworn before this board, I hold that the statements and testimony given are based on facts already in evidence but judged by Rating Team POST4/TMN not to be adequate to trigger the Doctrine of Reasonable Doubt and grant all benefits claimed. Appellant James R. Rogers hereby files this initial brief on the merits of the evidence of record. The parties will be referred to as follows: James R. Rogers will be identified as the *appellant*, Rating Officer Irene Dunn as *RO,* Decision Review Officer James Lincoln as *DRO*, Nurse Practitioner Nancy Drew as

continued on next page

continued from previous page

ARNP. The Appeal Officer will be *AO*. The Board of Veterans' Appeals will be referred to as the *BVA*. The Department of Veterans Affairs will be designated as the *VA*. The U.S. Court of Appeals for Veterans Claims will be referred to as *CAVC* or the *Court*.

The letter "N" will identify new evidence offered at the time of this hearing. The use of the letter "A" denotes evidence appended to this appeal copied from the claim file.

A Simple Introductory Statement

If this was a civil trial your attorney would give an opening statement as to the facts of your case for the benefit of the trial judge and the jury. The appellant, who is represented by a service representative, an attorney, or by himself, must make a good first impression. He or she must show that he or she was wronged by the VA and that the facts and evidence of record support his or her claim. Be aware that your introduction can make or break your appeal hearing. First impressions can never be duplicated. You only have one chance to make a good impression on the hearing judge.

Your goal in this administrative hearing is to persuade the hearing judge that you should prevail because the facts and evidence of record override the faulty conclusion reached by the Regional Office raters when they attempted to justify the denial of your claim. This point of view begins with a simple introductory paragraph in your statement of historical facts and should read something like this:

> This is an appeal resulting from the denial of a claim for coronary artery disease (CAD) and adjustment disorder with anxiety and depression by the Washington, D.C., Regional Office's adjudication team known as POST4/TMN. The evidence of record denotes that the claim was erroneously judged by POST4/TMN and that said team failed to comply with the laws and regulations that govern the process of adjudicating claims.

This short statement explains what you intend to prove and that your arguments are sufficient to prevail. You must argue each issue with confidence and with the assurance that your arguments are convincing and correct. An interesting bit of information I found on the Internet described an attorney's introduction to his client's lawsuit, which is applicable to your case:

> It is crucial for a party to get the judge and jury interested in his/her story, and doing so beginning with the opening statement goes a long way toward hooking the audience. If the opening is delivered in a boring, bland way, in monotone and without making eye contact, the audience, judge, jury, witnesses, and so on will quickly lose interest.

The person delivering the opening statement should speak clearly and confidently, look at the audience, and be passionate about the case. If the jury and judge see how much it means to an appellant to prevail in the lawsuit, they are more likely to be genuinely concerned about the outcome of the case and about how it will affect the claimant.

The opening statement should paint a complete picture of the case. It is important to present a clear theme and to do so in a straightforward manner that will neither confuse nor bore the decision makers. Appellants should make a statement that establishes why their position is correct and make that the focus of their opening argument and of their case as a whole. The purpose of the opening statement is only to prepare the court for what a claimant's arguments will be and to create a rapport with the court, inspiring the trust and sympathy of the decision maker.

STATEMENT OF HISTORICAL FACTS

The first step in preparing your statement of historical facts is to determine what you must prove to establish how the injuries or illnesses are related to military service. For example, you know that if you are claiming cardiovascular disease and depression with secondary anxiety, you want to show how work-related stress, high-decibel sounds, shift work, gum disease, long irregular work hours, high-fat diets, and near-death incidents are just a few of the factors that contribute to heart disease.

In the second step you want to emphasize what errors the VA made and who made them. Here you want to illustrate exactly what evidence of record was ignored or misinterpreted by the Rating Team, Decision Review Officer, the Appeals Officer, the C&P Examiner, and the Compensation Section Chief. All C&P physicians, physicians assistants, and nurse practitioners work under his medical status and direction.

Synopsis of Military Service

The example that follows illustrates the type of military duties the appellant performed during his twenty years in the air force. It provides the hearing judge with a verifiable picture of the stress and duties associated with the appellant's service. All of these duties included factors that contributed to the development of his heart disease.

> I served in the U.S. Air Force from April 1971 to September 1991 (A-1). I flew combat missions into North Vietnam in 1973 and in 1989 served in the capacity of Director of Personnel for an Air Force Security Wing headquartered in the Philippines. I was required to travel extensively throughout Southeast Asia. Unit locations were in Thailand, Philippines, Taiwan, South Korea, and Japan. I was awarded the Vietnam Service Medal with one bronze star, several Air Force Commendation Medals (A-2), and an Air Medal with one star.
>
> During my combat tour in Vietnam, I survived a crash landing in 1973 at Da Nang Air Base, South Vietnam, and later was temporarily

continued on next page

continued from previous page

grounded for a ruptured eardrum resulting from loss of pressurization (owing to flak damage to my F-4). Between 1973 and 1985 I was a F-4 and C-123 Aircraft Commander, I logged nearly 2,500 hours as an air force pilot (A-3). Stress as a TAC combat crew member caused me to be grounded several times as a result of chronic ulcers (A-4). During my flying years, I experienced many dangerous incidents resulting in occupational stress.

In response to a VA request for additional evidence, the Rating Board was made aware of

PSYCHOLOGIST SUSPENDED BY VAMC

For Saying "No" to Thirty-Minute C&P Evaluations

This story was headlined "Fight over VA Benefits Exposed" and ran in the *St. Petersburg Times* on September 6, 2005. The problem started when Dr. Dominique Thurire, director of Mental Health and Behavioral Sciences, decided thirty minutes was more than enough time to conduct mental examinations. The push to accelerate the processing time was the result of the backlog of pending psychological evaluations. Dr. Allen Fine stated he these incidents when I filed a sworn "Statement in Support of Claim" dated June 26, 2005. (See pages 21 A-7 to 21 A-10.)

Upon retirement from the air force, I was rated 40 percent disabled for ulcers and 20 percent for chronic prostatitis. In September 2005, I was rated 10 percent for bilateral tinnitus and 0 percent for bilateral hearing loss as a result of twenty-three years of daily exposure to noise (A-19). Following a two-year tour in Southeast Asia I served my final two years as a member of the 9th Air Force Inspector General's inspection staff. My duties involved inspecting

continued on next page

could not do a proper evaluation in thirty minutes. Thus he was consistently late in furnishing complete reports. His C&P supervisor moved to fire him; however the chief of staff overruled the decision and changed the punishment to a thirty-day suspension without pay. Dr. Fine appealed his suspension with the U.S. Merit Systems Protection Board, which reinstated him with full pay. On his return he was transferred out of the C&P unit for his inability to conform to hospital policy and failing to be a team player. Go to www.gulfwar vets.com/vetbenefits exposed.htm to read the complete story. ●

continued from previous page

> all personnel functions at air force bases, Air Force Reserve units, and Air National Guard bases east of the Mississippi River. This duty required me to travel four and a half days a week. This, like all of my previous assignments, was a high-stress assignment that was physically demanding. For nearly four years, my assignments did not permit me to be with my family.

You will note that in the appellant's statement, he inserted a series of tab letters and numbers that specifically relate to documents that supports his arguments. Tab (A-1) is proof of service, which confirms his combat duty and length of service. Tab (A-2) provides proof of his extensive travel through Southeast Asia. Tab (A-3) is verification of his flight records. Tab (A-4) introduces military hospital records dated 1977, which confirm ulcers owing to stress. Stress is one of the risk factors that contribute to heart disease. The appellant also provided medical proof that heart disease can take decades to develop before a heart attack occurs.

Military Medical Records Establish Heart Disease

Next, the appellant referenced active-duty medical records, which established that two years before retiring he was treated for symptoms of heart disease. Tab (A-6) is a copy of a military emergency room treatment record related to chest pain at Shaw Air Force Base in 1989. The following is how the appellant introduced this information in his statement of historical facts:

It was in 2004 that my cardiologist, who was looking for more historical medical background, asked me about health problems in the service. This inquiry prompted me to request copies of my hospital records from Shaw Air Force Base in South Carolina.

Both Drs. Vernon Smith and Ralph Sherman (cardiologists), upon reviewing the records, concurred that the early stages of heart disease

continued on next page

WHERE BUREAUCRACY RUNS AMOK

This is a harsh criticism of a system that has a responsibility to evaluate those who became injured or severely disabled because of an illness in service of his or her country. The appellant, James R. Rogers, was initially victimized by a harried nurse practitioner (who possessed neither a medical degree nor a medical specialization). She gave him an in-and-out-the-door examination and a final report all within a thirty-minute time frame. She was protecting her job and rushing through examinations every thirty minutes. As a result, her final report concluded that to grant service connection for cardiovascular disease would be purely speculative since there was no published medical thesis that stress, sound, gum disease, excessive work hours, and irregular work hours were all factors that cause heart disease. ●

continued from previous page

> were demonstrated in 1989 (A-15, A-16). Dr. Edward Powers, my primary care physician, having reviewed the records and the statements of both cardiologists, also concurred that a diagnosis of heart disease was present in 1990 and 1991 (A-17).
>
> It was not until this information was made known to me that I filed a claim for coronary artery disease (CAD) and adjustment disorder with anxiety and depressed mood secondary to heart disease. These underlying symptoms, which I experienced for more than three decades, were not sufficiently severe to alert me to seek medical care. Even the first heart attack I experienced, in 1995, did not alert me to the fact that my heart disease had its onset decades before.

The appellant obtained these hospital records from the National Personnel Records Center because the Regional Office failed to obtain them, even though the RO was made aware of their existence at the time of the application for benefits. There are several reasons for raising this point, one of which is to draw the hearing judge's attention to the fact the adjudication division ignored its duty to assist the claimant in obtaining all the records before the claim was rated. Where applicable, point out the inept manner in which the claim was processed. Your mission is to show the adjudication division's absence of creditability and impress the judge with your ability to evaluate the regulations and laws that govern the granting of benefits.

ISSUES ON APPEAL

Within the Department of Veterans Affairs there are two independent agencies that are empowered to deny your benefits. Both the Veterans Benefits Administration (which evaluates the claim) and the Veterans Health Administration (which evaluates medical aspects of the claim) often disregard rules, regulations, and laws passed by Congress to achieve their own agency agendas. A couple of interesting stories illustrate the importance of knowing how and why the systems work (see sidebars).

The appellant, James Rogers, identified the issue of medical incompetence as appealable when he received copies of all his records. Following are his commments:

ISSUE III
C&P Examiner lacked knowledge of heart disease resulting in a damaging and inaccurate medical evaluation.

ARNP Drew's lack of medical knowledge related to heart disease was detrimental to the appellant's claim. She wrote, "Opinion: Regarding current heart condition and its relation to the service, I cannot offer an opinion because such knowledge is not available in the medical literature, and any opinion would be speculation" (A-18).

continued on next page

continued from previous page

This rudimentary analysis by ARNP Drew was all the Rating Team members needed to deny the claim and for team POST4/MN to take a product credit. The Rating Team ignored 38 CFR §4.2 Interpretation of examination reports, 38 CFR §4.6 Evaluation of evidence, 38 CFR §4.19 Age in service-connected claims, and 38 CFR §4.23 Attitude of rating officers. It was not until this information was made known to the appellant that a claim was filed for coronary artery disease (CAD) and adjustment disorder with anxiety and depressed mood secondary to heart disease. These underlying symptoms that were experienced for more than three decades were not sufficiently severe to alert the appellant to seek medical care. Even the first heart attack the appellant experienced in 1995 did not alert him to the fact that his heart disease had its onset decades before.

To delegate the responsibility of a complicated medical examination, such as a heart examination, to a person who does not possess the basic knowledge of the causes and effects of cardiovascular disease is a disservice to all veterans. This is a deliberate violation of the published policy of the Department of Veterans Affairs by the hospital administration. A second-year medical student would know that exposure to high-decibel sounds, job stress, dental disease, fluctuating working hours, shortness of breath, chest pain, nocturnal leg cramps, shift work, and an inverted T wave captured on an EKG (A-8) are all early triggers and symptoms of heart disease. A medical student would also know that cardiovascular disease is a long-term condition: decades may elapse between the onset of the disease and a wake-up heart attack.

Had ARNP Drew had this basic knowledge of heart disease and reviewed the evidence of the record in its entirety, she would not have published a conclusion that "any opinion would be speculative" or that "such knowledge is not available in the medical literature." As far as the adjudication team (POST4/TMN) was concerned, they could deny his claim.

In *Doran v. Brown,* 6 Vet.App. 589 (1994), the CAVC ruled that the VA cannot refute expert medical advise proffered on the basis of its own unsubstantiated medical conclusion. Appeals Officers "must articulate a reason or basis for its decision." The Rating Officer devoted thirteen out of fifteen pages quoting 38 CFR §3.102, §3.159, §3.260, §3.303, §3.307, and §3.309, which state the rules that *might* apply before granting benefits.

The RO held that the disability must be *diagnosed* rather than *manifested* to 10 percent within one year following separation from the service. The claimant must introduce evidence that demonstrates the disease *manifested* to a degree of 10 percent two years prior to retirement.

The appellant provided the Appeals Team with more than thirty documents that clearly demonstrated a nexus between the genesis of cardiovascular disease and its presence prior to his retirement from the air force. The records also showed that the POST4/TMN team removed some of these documents and then shipped the claim file to an off-site storage location. Presumably, the expectation of the Appeals Team was that the claim file would be stored for a couple of years before being called up for review by the Board of Veterans' Appeals.

Had the appellant not filed a motion with the Board of Veterans' Appeals to be advanced on the list for a personal hearing because of his health and age, he might have died before the BVA addressed the issue. I think it is important at this point to note that the hearing judge agreed with the appellant on all arguments raised. The judge ruled that evidence and argument established service connection for the appellant's heart disease retroactively back to 2005, and he further stated that the Regional Office had no evidence to rebut the veteran's arguments.

Identify All Issues for the Hearing Judge

The examples so far in this chapter represent one way to present your arguments. You may have your own methods that work just as well. What is important is that you meet your objective of making each issue you discuss bullet proof. For every issue you identify, your argument should answer "who," "what," "where," and "when." Here is how appellant Rogers discussed one of his ten issues:

ISSUE III.
Supervising physician accepted conclusions at face value without challenging erroneous finding and conclusions by a nurse practitioner.

Dr. William T. Button, the C&P unit supervisor, committed a grave error by allowing ARNP Drew's C&P Evaluation to go forward with his approval to the Regional Office. It is inconceivable that a physician charged with the responsibility of reviewing all C&P Evaluations would allow a marginally qualified medical person to categorically state there was no medical literature to support the appellant's claim.

It is an accepted medical principle that cardiovascular disease can slowly destroy a person's heart and vascular system over decades. To permit such a finding to go forward unchallenged opens the door to questions of Dr. Button's medical competency (A-26). Had this supervisor reviewed the complete file as required by regulations and case law, he would have noted that two board-certified cardiologists and one board-certified primary care physician rendered findings contrary to those of the nurse practitioner. (Read *Skyler v. Brown*, 5 Vet.App. 146 (1993) and 38 CFR §4.70.)

continued on next page

continued from previous page

> By law and regulation, minimally qualified medical staff are required to work under the umbrella of a physician. For the VA, the hiring of medical staff with such limited experience is an effective method of cost reduction.

SUMMARY

You are now in the homestretch, and you will want one last chance to review for the hearing judge why he or she should grant the benefits. You want the summary not to come across as repetetive. The summary should be a concise recapitulation of the evidence introduced in your appeal to draw the hearing judge's attention to the relevant issues you discussed. Here is appellant Rogers's summary that contributed to his winning his appeal:

> SUMMARY
> For the reasons I have stated, a grievous error was committed when my claim was not adjudicated in compliance with the policies of the Department of Veterans Affairs and the intent of Congress. A series of administrative and procedural mistakes by members of Team POST4/TMN of the Washington, D.C., Regional Office and Washington, D.C., Medical Center contributed to my claim being denied erroneously. The timeline of events reveals a

mind-set that, once embedded, seems impossible to influence or reverse.

The actions that have been presented in this hearing have delayed a fair adjudication of the appellant's claim for more than two years:

ISSUE I.

This goal-driven process to clear claims as rapidly as possible with little time to reflect on the evidence is a disservice to all veterans and creates a high-casualty rate for veterans' claims.

No matter how thin the evidence might seem, the element of "Reasonable Doubt" must in every instance favor the veteran (see 38 CFR §4.3). There is no place in the decision process for an adjudicator's personal opinion when he or she adjudicates the claim (see 38 CFR §4.23).

ISSUE II.

ARNP Drew was trusted with the responsibility of completing a "thorough and contemporaneous examination." She demonstrated her inability to perform such an evaluation when she blatantly stated there were no medical studies, thesis, medical texts, or publications available to establish a nexus between the early onset of chronic heart disease and a full-blown heart attack.

continued on next page

continued from previous page

She stated for the record that she reviewed hundreds of pages of evidence, as well as documents that included medical opinions of board-certified cardiologists—all within a six-minute time frame—and concluded, "any opinion would be speculation." Exhibits A-20, A-21, A-22, and A-24 support the conclusion that she could not and did not perform at or above average in this case. To accept evidence from a person with such a shallow level of understanding is unconscionable.

ISSUE III.

The Rating Officer failed to obtain the appellant's complete records. As a consequence, the C&P Examiner did not review or consider appellant Rogers's complete medical history before signing off on the C&P report.

ISSUE IV.

Dr. Button, a licensed physician supervisor, signed off on ARNP Drew's report and therefore was equally culpable. He allowed a faulty and incomplete C&P report to move forward, one that contradicted three board-certified physicians diagnoses. This is inexcusable.

ISSUE V.

Failure of Rating Officer Christie to read all documented evidence submitted by the appellant and to challenge the results of the C&P

report violates 38 CFR §4.02. The examination must be reviewed in the light of the "whole recorded history and reconciliation of the various reports into a consistent picture so that the current rating may accurately reflect the elements of disability." In addition to an incomplete document review, Rating Officer Christie accepted the medical conclusion "such knowledge is not available in the medical literature, and any opinion would be speculation."

To permit a Rating Officer to disregard 38 CFR §4.6, Evaluation of evidence, without solid evidence to rebut the appellant's claim is grounds for reversal by the BVA. 38 CFR §4.6 states, "Every element in any way affecting the probative value to be assigned to the evidence in each individual claim must be thoroughly and conscientiously studied by the Rating Officer in the light of the established policies of the Department of Veterans Affairs to the end that decisions will be equitable and just as contemplated by the requirements of the law."

ISSUE VI.

The Regional Office failed to explain exactly why the evidence submitted by the appellant was not acceptable. The VA also must cite its reasons within the context of the original letter of denial to the claimant. The U.S. Court of Appeals for Veterans Claims has in case

continued on next page

continued from previous page

after case ruled that the "Rating Officer must articulate reasons and bases for apparent dismissal of records favorable to the veteran." (See *Willis v. Derwinski,* 1 Vet.App. 63 [1991], *Shaw v. Principi*, 3 Vet.App. 365 [1992], and *Wilson v. Derwinski*, 1 Vet.App. 139 [1991].) It is a decade and a half since the Court first issued the order that, when a claim is denied, the rating officer must explain in detail his or her rationale for dismissing evidence favorable to the veteran. To this day Rating Officers continue to ignore this order.

The appeal and Dr. Smith's letter were filed without response, and Rogers was notified that his appeal was certified to the Board of Veterans' Appeals for final disposition. Here again members of POST4/TMN ignored the appellant's rights by failing to issue a Supplemental Statement of the Case as required by 38 CFR §19.39.

ISSUE VII.

It is obvious the Appeals Officer deliberately ignored all the factors of record that cause chronic heart disease. Nowhere did he address the effects that exposure to high-decibel sounds, job stress, dental disease, fluctuating working hours, shortness of breath, chest pain, nocturnal leg cramps, shift work, and an inverted T wave captured on an EKG (A-8) were triggers and symptoms of heart disease in progress. It is important to note that the appellant made known to the Appeals Officer (A-28) that all these long-term medical factors stated above were the causation of my heart disease.

This case is an example of a rigidly executed denial that paid no heed to the law by all members of POST4/TMN. I respectfully submit these arguments in rebuttal to the denial of my claim for benefits based on arteriosclerosis heart disease and adjustment disorder with anxiety and depressed mood secondary to heart disease.

Respectfully,
James R. Rogers CSS 122-55 9502

THE APPEAL DECISION

If the BVA Decision Is "Yes"

If the Board of Veterans' Appeals rules in your favor, your quest is at an end. You won! However, I need to say one last time that if you or your representative do not put all your energy into researching the issues; obtaining solid evidence; identifying the errors the Rating Officer may have made; identifying any breach of laws, regulation, or court decisions; and putting it in a format that will keep the hearing judge focused and interested in your presentation, you will lose. You do not want the hearing judge to spend endless hours scouring a claim file or files that may be five or six inches thick to determine if the local Regional Office made any errors. The burden of proof is on you. If you say you injured your back, you have to find solid proof that this injury did in fact take place while you where on active duty.

If the BVA Decision Is "No"

If the BVA rules against you, you can take your case to the U.S. Court of Appeals for Veterans Claims. However, you need to take a good hard look at your case to see if you have a chance of winning before taking any action. Ask yourself, did I dot all the "I's" and cross all the "T's" when I presented my case before the Board of Veterans' Appeals? Next carefully review the reasons and bases the Board cited for why they did not grant you your benefits.

The law allows you to represent yourself but does not allow your Service Officer to plead your case before the CAVC. If you did not have an attorney, especially one specializing in VA appeals, now is the time to start looking for one. Here are some of the basics you should know concerning appealing to the CAVC:

a. You have 120 days to file a motion to appeal the BVA decision commencing the day the decision letter is dated.
b. There is a $50 filing fee payable to the court.
c. The attorney will charge a fee to represent you before the Court. The cost is a variable in that it may be derived by the number of hours he or she will spend preparing your appeal. Alterna-

tively, the attorney may charge a flat rate that may include all associated costs and fees associated with the appeal.

d. You may be able to locate an attorney who will take your case pro bono, meaning he or she will not charge you for his or her time.
e. Many attorneys will not charge you to evaluate the merits of your case.
f. Take a copy of the appeal you filed with the Board of Veterans' Appeals to the attorney along with all evidence that supports your arguments. Make certain you take along all correspondence from the Board of Veterans' Appeals with you when you meet to discuss the possibilities of your appeal to the Court.

During the past decade, the CAVC has reshaped the way the Board of Veterans' Appeals decides its issues. It is in most cases in harmony with the laws and regulations that govern veteran benefits. Decisions to reverse Board of Veterans' Appeals decisions are at an all time low. That is not to say that the BVA no longer makes legal errors when deciding appeals. You need someone who is trained to sniff out these technical errors that might go unnoticed. As I said earlier, you have hundreds of thousands of dollars over your lifetime riding on your appeal. You need the best of the best to get what is lawfully yours.

RESOURCES:
HOW TO FIND WHAT YOU NEED

The number of search engines available to a researcher is numbered in the thousands. If you are searching for institutions, such as government agencies or departments, universities, data banks, private or public organizations, the federal court system, or medicine or medical studies, or locating individuals, you will find that many of these sites have search engines to assist you.

Online Sources

General Research

AltaVista: www.altavista.com/
Ask: www.ask.com
Dogpile: www.dogpile.com/
Google: www.google.com/search
Microsoft Network: www.msn.com/
Yahoo: www.yahoo.com/

Government Archives

Department of Defense: http://defenselink.mil/sites/
- Air Force: www.af.mil/
- Army: http://army.mil/

Coast Guard: www.uscg.mil/
Marine Corps: http://usmc.mil/marinelink
Navy: www.navy.mil/swf/index.asp
Department of State: www.state.gov
Records in the National Archives: www.archives.gov/research/state-dept/
Department of Veterans Affairs: www.va.gov
Board of Veterans Appeals: www.va.gov/vbs/bva/
General Counsel Decisions: www.va.gov/OGC
VA Manual M21-1MR:http:/www.warms.vba.va.gov/M21_1MR.html
National Archives and Record Administration www.archives.gov/veterans/research/
NPRC: www.archives.gov/st-louis/military-personnel/
38 CFR Parts 3 and 4: www.vba.va.gov/bln/21/Reference/

Law

Federal Circuit Court of Appeals: http://cases.justia.com/us-court-of-appeals/circuit/cafc
U.S. Court of Appeals for Veterans Claims: www.vetapp.uscourts.gov/

Libraries

Library of Congress: www.loc.gov/rr/research-centers.html
New York City Library: www.nypl.org/
West Point Library: http://usmalibrary.usma.edu/

Medical Research

American Cancer Society: www.cancer.org

American Heart Association: www.americanheart.org/
Center for Disease Control: www.cdc.go
Diabetes Type Two: www.januvia.com
National Institutes of Health: http://nems.nih.gov/index.cfm

Military History

Air Force Historical Research Agency: www.au.af. mil/au/afhra
Army Center Military History: www.history.army.mil/
Marine Corps Historical Center: www.history.usmc.mil/
Naval Historical Center: www.history.navy.mil/

Periodicals

Newspapers

Associated Press: www.ap.org
Chicago Tribune: www.chicagotribune.com/
New York Times: www.nytimes.com/
Los Angeles Times: www.latimes.com
Reuters News wire service: www.reuters.com
Washington Post: www.washingtonpost.com/
Washington Times: www.washingtontimes.com/

Military Publishing Companies

Army Times Publishing Company, Inc.
Classified Department
6883 Commercial Drive
Springfield, VA 22159
703-750-8915
www.atpco.com

Stars & Stripes
Business Office
PO Box 187
Thurmont, MD 21788
www.estripes.com

Military Magazines

Air Force Magazine
1501 Lee Highway
Arlington, VA 22209-1198
www.afa.org/magazinelmagz.html
703-247-5800

American Legion Magazine
Advertising Editor Assistance
PO Box 1055
Indianapolis, IN 46206
www.legion.org/publicationslpubs_mag_index.htm
317-630-1200

DVA Magazine
PO Box 14301
Cincinnati, OH 45250-030 1
www.dav.org/magazine

Leatherneck
Mail Call Editor
PO Box 1775
Quantico, VA 22134
www.mca-marines.org/Leatherneck/lneck.html

Military Officer Association of America
Editor

201 N. Washington Street
Alexandria, VA 22314
703-683-1480
www.moaa.org/Locator/Default.asp

Naval Affairs
Attn: Editor
Fleet Reserve Association
125 N. West Street
Alexandria, VA 22314-2754
www.fra.org/navalaffairsl

NCOA Journal
Noncommissioned Officers Association
1065 IH 35N
San Antonio, TX 78233
www.ncoausa.org
1-800-662-2620

VFW Magazine
Advertising Editor
Veterans of Foreign Wars Building
406 West 34th Street, Suite 219
Kansas City, MO 64111
www.vfw.org/magazine
816-756-3390

Government Archives

NARA
National Archives and Records Administration
1700 Pennsylvania Avenue NW
Washington, DC 20408

National Archives II
8601 Adelphi Road
College Park, MD 20740-6001

Federal Publications

You can find 38 CFR at the following websites:
www.gpoaccess.gov/ecfr
www.vba.va.gov/bln/21/Reference/
http://thomas.loc.gov

The *Federal Register* is available at:
www.archives.gov/federal-register/
www.access.gpo.gov/su_doc/aces/aces 140.html

Title 38 USC can be found at:
http://uscode.house.gov/title38.htm
www.law.cornell.edu/uscode/38

Case law can be found at:
www.fedcir.gov (U.S. Court of Appeals for the Federal Circuit)
www.va.gov/vbs/bva
www.vetapp.uscourts.gov (U.S. Court of Appeals for Veterans Claims)

Military Historical Records Centers

National Personnel Records Center—Military Personnel Records Division
9700 Page Avenue
St. Louis, MO 63 132-5100

Veterans Affairs

Toll Free: 1-800 827-1000

Local: 1-314-538-4500 (NPRC central office, St. Louis)

Military Historical Archives

Air Force History Support Office
AFHSO/HOS
Reference and Analysis Division
200 McCord Street, Box 94
Bolling AFB, DC 20332-1111
www.airforcehistory.hq.af.mil

Department of the Navy
9th and M Streets SE
Washington, DC 20374
202-433-3396 (Personal Papers Collection)
202-433-3439 (Archives Section)
www.history.usmc.mil/

Naval Historical Center
901 M Street SE
Washington, DC 20374-5060

Naval Historical Center
Washington Navy Yard
805 Kidder Breese Street SE
Washington Navy Yard, DC 20374-5060
www.history.navy.mil/

U.S. Air Force
Air Force Support Office
500 Duncan Avenue, Box 94
Bolling AFB, DC 20332-1111
202-404-2264

U.S. Army Center of Military History
Attn: DAMH-MD
103 Third Avenue
Ft. McNair, DC 20319-5058
202-761-5444 (fax)
www.armyhistoryfnd.org/info.htm

U.S. Marine Corps
Reference Section
Marine Corps Historical Center
Building 58
Washington Navy Yard
Washington, DC 20374-5060

Special Military Searches

Archives II Textual Reference Branch
National Archive and Records Administration
8601 Adelphi Road
College Park, MD 20740-6001

Freedom of Information Act and Privacy Division
Hoffman Building I, Room 1146
2461 Eisenhower Avenue
Alexandria, VA 22331-0301

U.S. Army Center of Military History
103 Third Avenue
Ft. McNair, DC 20319-5058

U.S. Army Institute of Heraldry
9325 Gunston Road
Room S-112
Fort Belvoir, VA 22060-5579

Department of Defense

To request proof of participation in a non-U.S. nuclear test.

U.S. Air Force
Commander, Non-flight Duties
Department of the Air Force
Armstrong Laboratory
AL/OEBS, Bldg. 140
Brooks AFB, TX 78235-5500
410-536-2378

U.S. Air Force
HQAFTAC/ICO
Flight Missions
1030 South Highway AlA
Patrick AFB, FL 32925-3002
407-494-6867

U.S. Army
Chief, U.S. Army Ionizing Radiation Dosimetry Center
Attn: AMXTM-SR-D
PO Box 14063
Lexington, KY 40512-4063
606-293-3646

U.S. Coast Guard
Commandant (G-KSE)
U.S. Coast Guard
2100 2nd Street SW
Washington, DC 20593
202-267-1368

U.S. Navy and U.S. Marine Corps
Officer in Charge
Naval Dosimetry Center
Navy Environmental Health Center Detachment
Bethesda, MD 20889-5614
301-295-5426

Branches of Service

To request occupational radiation exposure documents

Department of Energy
Department of Energy-OHRE (EH-8)
1000 Independence Avenue, SW
Washington, DC 20585
202-586-8800

Overseas Citizens Services
U.S. Department of State
2201 C Street NW
Washington, DC 20520
1-202-647-5225

U.S. Air Force
Department of the Air Force
USAF Occupational Health Laboratory (AFSC)
Brooks AFB, TX 78235-5501

U.S. Army
Chief, U.S. Army Ionizing Radiation Dosimetry Center
Attn: AMXTM-CE-DCR
Lexington, KY 40511-5102
606-239-3249

U.S. Coast Guard
Commandant U.S. Coast Guard
Attn: Mr. James Veazey
2100 2nd Street SW
Washington, DC 20593-0001

U.S. Navy and U.S. Marine Corps
Officer in Charge
Naval Dosimetry Center
Navy Environmental Health Center
Bethesda, MD 20889-5614
301-295-5426

INDEX

ABOUT THE AUTHOR

John Roche's involvement as a veteran's advocate began nine years before he retired from the U.S. Air Force. His VA actions on behalf of retired military personnel came to the attention of the St. Petersburg Regional Office's adjudication officer when, as a casualty assistance officer, he successfully argued for a widow that her retired Air Force officer husband's accidental death in the county jail was service-connected.

Immediately after leaving the air force, Roche joined the VA Regional Office adjudication division as a claims specialist. During the three years that he was with the VA, he completed its 1,560-hour formal training program and gained considerable insight into why so many claims were denied. Veterans did not know how to prove their claims; they relied on the VA to do it for them.

His decision to leave the VA was fostered by policies that contradicted the reason he accepted the job. Since leaving the VA, Roche has used his knowledge of the system to help more than forty thousand clients during the past thirteen years as a county service officer. Health reasons caused him to step down as an active veteran's advocate with the county service in 1996.

Roche is a published writer specializing in veteran's

issues and has four forthcoming books on the subject. He has written five books focusing on how to get claims approved. His books have introduced him to veterans from all over the United States who have had legitimate claims denied.

Mr. Roche is a lifetime member of the Disabled American Veterans, National Association for Uniformed Services, and the Military Officers Association of America. He is also a member of Congressman Michael Bilirakis's advisory board. He lives in Palm Harbor, Florida.